Special Event Graphics

Designing for seminars, festivals, fund-raisers, exhibitions and other special events

P·I·E BOOKS

Special Event Graphics

First published in Japan in 1992 by:

P·I·E BOOKS

Villa Phoenix Suite 407, 4-14-6, Komagome,

Toshima-ku,Tokyo 170, Japan

Tel: 03-3949-5010 Fax: 03-3949-5650

ISBN 4-938586-35-5

First published in Germany in 1992 by:

Nippan

Nippon Shuppan Hanbai Deutschland GmbH

Krefelder Str. 85

D-4000 Düsseldorf 11 (Heerdt)

GERMANY

Tel: 0211- 5048089 Fax: 0211- 5049326

ISBN 3-910052-24-X

Printed in Japan

The design used for the front cover was provided by
Crosby Associates, Liska and Associates,
Maria Grillo, Samata Associates,
Essex Two, Concrete and Influx

Event Name	イベント名称
Country of Work	制作国
Year of Completion	制作年
Creative Director	クリエイティブ ディレクター
Art Director	アートディレクター
Designer	デザイナー
Photographer	フォトグラファー
Illustrator	イラストレーター
Artist	アーティスト
Design Firm	デザインファーム
Client	クライアント
Item	アイテム

Editorial Notes:

Detailes are given for multiple item inclusions for one
event and for items which have some unusual aspect.
アイテムは数が多いもの、特種な形状のものに表記した。

Event graphics which were produced from 1985 through
1992 are included in this book. The words "Company
Limited" and "Incorporated"have been omitted from book.
本書は1985年から1992年までのイベントグラフィックス
を掲載対象としている。本文クレジット中、会社名につ
いては株式会社、Company Limited, Incorporated 等の表
記を省略した。

Contents

はじめに

人が集まって充実した時間を共有する――イベントには集まる人や目的によって様々な形式があり、区別されます。例えばある一つのテーマとスピリットに基いて開催される国際規模のエキスポやフェスティバル、地方自治体や業界レベルのコンベンションやトレードショー、企業や個人レベルのセレブレーションで行われるセミナーやパーティ、またはショービジネスとしてのオペラ、演劇、コンサート等タイプは数多く、目的や規模によって、それぞれルールも性質も全く異なっています。一般に業界レベル以上の比較的大きなイベントになると、そのビジュアル・アイデンティティは主催者側と参加者側の距離感が影響してとらえにくくなりますが、企業や個人レベルのイベントとなると主催者側のポリシーが比較的スムーズに伝わる傾向にあるようです。

イベントにおけるデザインを考えてみると、それは限られた時間と空間の中で一つのトータルなイメージを表現するために不可欠なものであり、イベントの成否にも大きく関係してくるものとしてとらえることができます。ディスプレイデザインやサウンドビジュアルと同様にイベントのためのグラフィック・アイテムは、限られた時間のなかである一つのストーリーを展開しています。ポスターやチラシ、あるいはインビテーションカードは、来たる出来事のアナウンスメントとインフォメーションの役割をもち、プログラム、ガイドブック、パンフレット等は内容の詳細を示唆するパートとして、参加者のみが手にすることのできるものです。そして記念品やスーベニール、Ｔ－シャツやノベルティグッズに至っては、そのイベントをより印象づけるものとして存在し、イベント閉幕の後までも残されるアイテムと言えるでしょう。イベントの多彩さと合わせて、グラフィック・アイテムのコンビネーションパターンもバラエティに富んでいます。これらのデザイニングは主催者のポリシーと、メインとなるキャラクターあるいはアーティスト、時には商品の個性やコンセプト、そしてデザイナーのセンスが共通の理解のうえに行われることが理想的です。デザインは今や独自のイマジネーションだけの所産ではないことは、既にそれぞれのデザインワークのなかで周知のこととは思われますが、イベントのためのグラフィックスを見ると、特にその事実を痛感させられます。一つのイベントに携わる様々なスタンドポイントの人々が、それぞれの見地からのデザインに関するビジョンを持っていることと、それぞれの技術、研究、分析に対して客観的な配慮とグローバルな視点からの明確な見解があることからスタートして、各必要スペックがきれいに調和されるトータルワークであるほど、質の高いグラフィックデザインがクリエイトされるのではないでしょうか。

本書は、世界各地で毎日行われている多種多様なイベントのためのデザインを紹介しています。グラフィック・アイテムの似ているもの、そのコンビネーションパターンの類似するものを明快に見せる手段として、イベントの内容で分類してみました。例えばセミナーやコンベンションに使用されるグラフィック・アイテムと、ミュージアムやギャラリーでのエキシビションにおけるグラフィック・アイテムは異なっていますし、それぞれ別のカラーを放っています。本書は一つのイベントにおける数種類のグラフィック・アイテムを可能なかぎり幅広く掲載することで、そのイベントのビジュアルワールドが拡がることを試みていますが、より効果的なデザインのみをセレクトしているため、中には１アイテムの掲載もあります。優れた作品の一つ一つ、そしてディテールを見ることから、それらをジョイントしてまた新たなイマジネーションを構築していくプロセスは、本書を御覧いただく読者の方に与えられた課題でもあります。

'90年に入り国際情勢の変化のうちに、世紀末時代を迎えています。あらゆるイベントの姿、形も社会状況やライフスタイルの変化に呼応して大きく変わってきているようです。メセナに代表されるアーティスティックなイベントやCI戦略の一環としての企業の文化的プロモーションが積極的に頭角を現してきています。また恒例となっている地域のフェスティバルやスポーツイベント等も、脱物質主義や観念主義等の時代の流れに合わせて見直し、改良され少しずつ変容してきているようです。企業や社会にもアイデアが要求される今日の傾向であるゆえ、イベントの企画立案と、ビジュアル部分でのトータル・クリエイティブワークに求められるのは、正当かつ有意義なプランニングではないでしょうか。

そのような時代のなかでイベントを語る場合、顕著に浮上してきている出来事として次に挙げる三つをはずすことはできません。まず一つは、エイズ防止のためのキャンペーン・イベント。二つめに世界経済のアンバランスや数々の問題から生じた途上国の子供たちに向けたチャリティー・イベント。三つめに地球環境保全を考えるキャンペーン・イベント。これらは数あるイベントの中でも、明確な目的意識をもって構成されるものと言えます。そのグラフィックデザインに関しては、本書でも数作品を掲載していますが、利益主義でないがゆえに、よりメンタルな意味での崇高さが漂い、メッセージ色の強い色彩を放っています。実際このようなテーマを支援し運動を遂行するノン・プロフィットの組織や団体も数多く登場している現状を考えると、この種のイベントは今後さらに増えていくと思われます。そしてデザインにおいてもビジネスライクな制約のない、より自由な発想のもとに制作するかつてないビジュアルワークが期待されています。

イベントのためのグラフィックスは、制作に関わる人々や参加者はもちろん、目にする多くの人々がそのビジュアルコミュニケーションを認識するのと同時に、出来事に対しての共感、連帯意識、反感等の感情の違いはあるけれども、ある種の'喜び'や'楽しみ'をもたらすものであってほしいと考えます。

ピエ・ブックス 編集部

Preface

Events at which people gather together to share an enriching experience can be classified according to their stated goals and the participants they target. These include events of international scope, such as expos and world fairs, which are usually conceived with a unified theme; conventions and trade shows organized by local government or industry; corporate seminars; and, finally, private parties. In addition, we cannot overlook artistic performances, such as operas, plays, and concerts. In short, there is a great diversity in the types of public events, and each one has its own unique characteristics.

Generally speaking, the larger the event, the greater the distance between the organizers and the participants. Thus, the producers of a large event will find it more difficult to convey a clear visual identity. With smaller events, held by corporations or local citizens groups, the organizers' program tends to be communicated relatively easily.

When we consider the design problems related to the promotion of events, it is obvious that strong, integrated design is absolutely essential to present an easily grasped, concrete image of the concept in the limited time and space available. Ultimately, the power of the visual components will largely determine an event's success or failure. Just as with displays and audiovisual compositions, the graphic components created for an event must tell their story in a very limited time frame. Posters, handouts, and invitations announce and describe forthcoming events, while programs, guidebooks, and pamphlets give more in-depth information to the participants. Finally, souvenirs, T-shirts, and novelties serve as more lasting reminders, long after the event has passed.

Reflecting the diversity of the events themselves, the graphic components can be combined in an infinite variety of ways. Ideally, these components will be designed through a collaborative process, involving the organizers and artists, where all taking part have a shared understanding of the goals and style of the event. Whatever the main focus of the event may be, it has to be expressed not only in a unique manner but also in one that is clearly understood by everyone involved.

As we all know, good design is not the result of imagination alone. One need only look at individual pieces of work to see that. This becomes even more apparent when we look at event-related graphics. The various people involved in the production of a particular event have differing views and expectations of design. Each person's contribution has to be evaluated objectively, so that, in the end, there emerges a clear consensual conception of the relevant issues. That is the starting point from which a true collaborative process can be launched. The more harmonized and neatly executed the various specifications are, the higher quality will be the graphic design created.

This book features designs created for the full range of events that are taking place all over the world every day. We have classified the entries according to the type of event, so that we can introduce related graphic challenges and similar patterns of graphic design in a way that is easy to follow. An illustration of the diversity in this field of design is to contrast the graphic components that are used for seminars and conventions and those used for museum and gallery exhibitions.

We have tried to encompass the entire visual world of each event by featuring the widest possible range of graphic components for each. In some categories, however, limitations of space have meant that we can only show one item per event.

It is the happy task of readers to discover each of these outstanding artworks in detail, and then put them together to add new dimensions to their imagination.

Now that we have embarked into the nineties, we have already reached the turn of the twentieth century. It is a time of momentous change, both on the international and domestic scene. Events, both in format and in philosophical approach, are changing dramatically in response to new social circumstances and lifestyles. The funding of artistic events by corporations is beginning to emerge as a powerful new cultural force. Annual or periodic festivals and sports events are changing too, reflecting a shift from materialism to idealism. Thus, traditional events have been reviewed and reinterpreted for a new age.

In today's world, even corporations are expected to hold altruistic values. What is required of event planning, therefore, and what must be reflected in the creative, visual products related to events, is a very fine balance between persuasion and moral rectitude. The types of events that immediately come to mind are fundraisers in the campaign against AIDS and for the victims of poverty in developing countries, and events promoting greater awareness of environmental issues. The pieces of graphic design created for these events included in this volume express intellectual and spiritual values that makes them utterly non-commercial. Above all, the designs themselves, to say nothing of the contents, convey a compelling sense of purpose.

Currently, many non-profit organizations are emerging to support and promote various civic causes. Thus, this type of event is likely to increase. From this climate of heightened activity we can expect to see completely new types of visual works. Freed from the narrow confines of the profit motive, designers can be expected to stretch the boundaries of the known visual world.

Event-related graphics are a medium through which the producers of an event can convey their ideas and feelings to the participants or to those exposed to the graphics by chance in a public space. Naturally, everyone has his or her own opinion about each event. Some may be sympathetic, others neutral or even hostile to the atated goal of an event. The graphics, however, should convey the excitement and sheer joy of focusing the energy of so many people or a single occasion.

P·I·E BOOKS

Vorwort

Ereignisse, bei denen Menschen zu einem konstruktiven Zweck zusammenkommen, sehen je nach Menschtyp, der angesprochen werden soll, und Absicht der Veranstalter unterschiedlich aus. Wir können alle Ereignisse entsprechend einordnen. Es gibt Ereignisse auf internationaler Ebene, wie z. B. Messen oder Weltausstellungen,die gewöhnlich unter einem einheitlichen Thema und in einem einheitlichen Geist gestaltet werden. Es gibt Tagungenund Handelsmessen, die auf der Ebene von Gemeindeverwaltungenoder örtlicher Industrie organisiertwerden; Seminare, die von Unternehmen abgehalten werdenund schließlich private Anlässe. Darüber hinaus gibt es Vorstellungen zur Unterhaltung der Öffentlichkeit, wie oper, Theater, Konzerte und so weiter. Kurz, es gibt zahlreiche verschiedene Ereignisarten, und alle habensehr unterschiedliche Merkmale.

Allgemein gilt, je größer das Ereignis, um so größer die Entfernung zwischen Veranstaltern und Teilnehmern.Bei Großereignissen wird es also schwieriger, eine klare visuelle Identität zu vermitteln. Bei kleineren von Vereinen oder auch Ortsbewohnern veranstalteten Ereignissen läßt sich des Programm des Veranstalters gewöhnlich verhältnismäßig leicht vermitteln.

Betrachten wir die mit diesen Ereignissen verbundenen Design-Probleme, so ist offensichtlich, daß starkes, integriertes Design absolut notwendig ist, um in begrenzter Zeit und auf begrenztem Raum ein konkretes Bild des Konzeptes zu präsentieren. Die Kraft der visuellen Darstellung wird weitgehend über Erfolg oder Mißerfolg eines Ereignisses entscheiden. Wie bei Ausstellungsmaterial und audiovisuellen Kompositionen enthält auch die Anordnung für ein Ereignis angefertigter graphischer Darstellungen eine Art Schilderung, die ihre Geschichte in einem sehr begrenzten Zeitraum erzählen muß. Plakate, Handzettel und Einladungskarten dienen der Ankündigung und Information über bevorstehende Ereignisse, während Programme, Führer und Broschüren für den Besucher nähere Einzelheiten über das Ereignis enthalten. Schließlich soll durch Momentos, Souvenirs, T-Shirts und Neuheiten der Gesamteindruck des Ereignisses auf dauerhafte Weise unterstützt werden; diese Erinnerungen bleiben uns noch lange nach dem Ereignis erhalten.

Da die graphischen Elemente die Vielfalt der Ereignisse selbst widerspiegeln, gibt es eine unendliche Vielzahl von Möglichkeiten, zu denen sie kombiniert werden können. Idealerweise werden die Graphiken im Wege eines Gemeinschaftsverfahrens entworfen, durch die Veranstalter und Künstler ein ungehindertes gemeinsames Verständnis von Stil und Zielen des Ereignisses erhalten. mag, er muß einzigartige Merkmale haben, die von jedem Beteiligten klar verstanden werden.

Wie wir alle wissen, ist gutes Design nicht allein das Ergebnis von Phantasie. Man braucht sich nur einige einzelne Stücke anzusehen, um das zu erkennen. Wenn wir uns die für Ereignisse entworfene Graphiken ansehen, wird dies noch offensichtlicher. Die verschiedenen an einem Ereignis beteiligten Menschen haben im Hinblick auf Design unterschiedliche Auffassungen und deutlich verschiedene Vorstellungen. Die Fertigkeiten, Forschungs-, Untersuchungs- und Analysearbeit eines jeden müssen berücksichtigt und objektiv ausgewertet werden. Das Endergebnis müßte eine klare Vorstellung des Themas von einem allgemeinen Standpunkt aus gesehen sein. Das ist der Ausgangspunkt, von dem aus ein wirkliches Gemeinschaftsverfahren aufgenommen werden kann. Je mehr die verschiedenen erforderlichen Spezifikationen aufeinander abgestimmt und je sorgfältiger sie ausgeführt sind, um so hochwertiger wird das geschaffene Graphikdesign sein.

Dieses Buch zeigt Designs für eine Vielzahl von Ereignissen der Art, die täglich überall auf der Welt stattfinden. Wir haben diese Ereignisse entsprechend ihrem Inhalt klassifiziert, so daß damit verbundene graphische Herausforderungen und ähnliche Muster graphischer Darstellungen in leicht zu verfolgender Weise gezeigt werden können. Graphische Darstellungen zum Beispiel für Seminare und Tagungen unterscheiden sich stark von denen für Museums- und Galerieausstellungen. Sie haben unterschiedliche Tonalwerte.

Wir haben versucht, die gesamte visuelle Welt eines jeden Ereignisses durch die weitestmögliche Palette graphischer Darstellungen zu umfassen. Auf der anderen Seite ist, da unsere Graphikherausgeber berüchtigt wählerisch im Hinblick darauf sind, was in dieses Buch aufgenommen werden darf, in einigen Fällen nur eine Darstellung zu einem Ereignis abgebildet.

Unser Leser hat die schöne Aufgabe, sich jedes dieser Super-Kunstwerke im kleinsten Detail anzusehen und sie alle anschließend zu neuen Dimensionen seiner Vorstellung zusammenzusetzen.

Nun, da wir uns mitten in den 90er Jahren befinden, haben wir uns in gewisser Hinsicht bereits auf den Jahrhundertwechsel eingestellt. Dies ist eine Zeit bedeutungsvoller Veränderung sowohl auf internationaler Ebene als auch daheim. Die Ereignisse scheinen sich sowohl in Struktur als auch im philosophischen Lösungskonzept als Reaktion auf die sich verändernden sozialen Verhältnisse und Lebensweisen der Menschen drastisch zu verändern. Künstlerische Ereignisse, wie ein Methena-Konzert und kulturelle Veranstaltungen von Vereinen bilden sich allmählich zu mächtigen kulturellen Kräften heraus. Jährliche oder regelmäßige Feste und Sportveranstaltungen verändern sich ebenfalls. Sie reflektieren die Tendenzen unserer Zeit hin auf Konzeptualismus und weg von Materialismus. Traditionelle Ereignisse wurden daher mit neuen Augen überdacht und für ein neues Zeitalter neu interpretiert.

Es gibt heute einen Trend, bei dem selbst Vereine altruistische Werte beibehalten müssen. Was daher bei Ereignisplanung benötigt wird und was in dem kreativen, visuellen Produkt in Verbindung mit Ereignissen widergespiegelt werden muß, ist eine sehr feine Ausgewogenheit von überzeugender Technik und Rechtschaffenheit.

Wenn wir von Ereignissen vor einem solchen Hintergrund sprechen, denkt man sofort speziell an drei Typen. Erstens: Ereignisse in Verbindung mit der Anti-AIDS-Kampagne. Zweitens: Humanitäre Ereignisse, die veranstaltet werden, um die Not der Kinder in den Entwicklungsländern lindern zu helfen, in denen Ungleichgewichte in der Gesamtwirtschaft verheerende Auswirkungen haben. Drittens: Kampagnen-Ereignisse zur Förderung des Umweltschutzes. Dies sind unter vielen anderen die Ereignistypen, die eine klare Absicht verfolgen. Dieses Buch zeigt verschiedene Graphik-Designdarstellungen in Verbindung mit diesen Ereignissen. Wie Sie sehen werden, besitzen sie einen unverkennbar hohen intellektuellen sind. Die Designs selbst, ganz zu schweigen von den Inhalten, vermitteln sehr starke Zielvorstellungen.

Derzeit tauchen zahlreiche nicht gewinnorientierte Organisationen zur Unterstützung und Veranstaltung der verschiedenen bürgerlichen Anlässe auf. Die Anzahl derartiger Ereignisse wird daher wahrscheinlich zunehmen. Aus diesem Klima erhöhter Aktivität können wir visuelle Befreit von den recht engen Grenzen des Gewinnmotivs, werden die Desiger voraussichtlich die Grenzen der bekannten visuellen Welt überschreiten.

Ereignis-Graphiken werden zu einem Medium, durch das die Veranstalter des Ereignisses denen, die an dem Ereignis teilnehmen oder anderen, die die Grahpiken zufällig an einem öffentlichen Ort sehen, Überzeugungen oder Ansichten übermitteln. Natürlich hat jeder seine eigenen Gefühle über jedes stattfindende Ereignis. Manche stehen der Kernabsicht eines gegebenen Ereignisses vielleicht wohlwollend, andere dagegen neutral oder sogar feindlich gegenüber. Die Graphiken sollten trotzdem die Begeisterung und reine Freude vermitteln, die Energie so vieler Menschen auf einen einzigen Anlaß zu konzentrieren.

P·I·E BOOKS

AIGA 1991 NATIONAL CONFERENCE
"LOVE, MONEY, POWER:
THE HUMAN EQUATION"
全国会議 AIGA 1991
"LOVE, MONEY, POWER:
THE HUMAN EQUATION"

USA 1991

Creative Director

Bart Crosby

Design Firms

Crosby Associates

Liska and Associates

Maria Grillo

Samata Associates

Essex Two

Concrete

Influx

Client

**AIGA
(The American Institute of
Graphic Arts)**

Item

1. Poster
2. Schedule & Registration
3 Survey
4. Brochure
5. Invitation card
6. Ticket
7. Party invitation
8. Sticker

1

2

AIGA / MN DESIGN CAMP
デザインキャンプ AIGA / MN

USA 1989

Art Director

Daniel Olson & Kobe

Designer

Daniel Olson & Kobe

Copywriter

Chuck Carlson

Design Firm

Charles S. Anderson Design

Client

AIGA Minnesota

**THE NATIONAL CHURCH YOUTH
CONVENTION "FRONTLINE"**
全国教会青年コンベンション
"FRONTLINE"

USA 1992

Art Director

John Sayles

Designer

John Sayles

Illustrator

John Sayles

Copywriter

Wendy Lyons

Design Firm

Sayles Graphic Design

Client

Open Bible Churches

3

4

4

4

FOOD SERVICES OF AMERICA
"BOLDLY INTO TOMORROW"
CONFERENCE CAMPAIGN
アメリカ食品サービスの
売り手と顧客との協力会議
"BOLDLY INTO TOMORROW"

USA 1992

Art Director

Jack Anderson

Designers

Jack Anderson

Jani Drewfs

Cliff Chung

David Bates

Brian O'Neill

Illustrators

David Bates

Brian O'Neill

Copywriter

Food Services of America

Design Firm

Hornall Anderson Design Works

Client

Food Services of America

Item

1.Folder,Binder,Name tag
2.Invitation card
3.Plaque
4.Background disply

THE INTERNATIONAL CONGRESS FOR
CHILDRENS THEATRE "ASSITEJ"
子供劇場の国際会議 "ASSITEJ"

AUSTRALIA 1987

Art Director

Barrie Tucker

Designers

Barrie Tucker

Mark Janetzki

Design Firm

Barrie Tucker Design

Client

**Carclew Youth Performing
Arts Center**

SEMINARS & CONVENTIONS

"ICOGRADA MONTRÉAL 1991"
グラフィック デザイン協会国際会議
"ICOGRADA MONTRÉAL 1991"

CANADA 1990

Art Director

Mark Timmings

Designer

Daniel Lohnes

Photographer

Optima Photographie

Copywriter

Andrew Muir

Design Firm

Turquoise Design

Client

ICOGRADA Montréal 1991

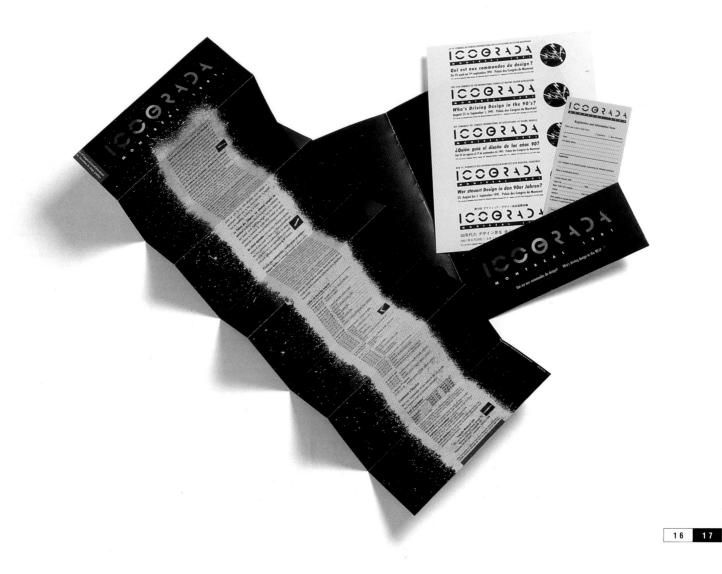

**PROMOTION OF CONGRESS
"AP! 63"**
プロモーション
"AP! 63"

ITALY 1992

Designer

Piermario Ciani

Client

Vittore Baroni

Item
1 Pamphlet
2 Post card
3 Record

**PROMOTION OF A COMMUNITY EVENT
"NETWORKER CONGRESS"**
地域社会イベントプロモーション
"NETWORKER CONGRESS"

ITALY 1992

Designer

Piermario Ciani

Client

Hans R. Fricker

Item
1. Letterhead
2. Sticker
3. Sticker
4. Postcard
5. Name tag
6. Invitation sheet
7. Sticker

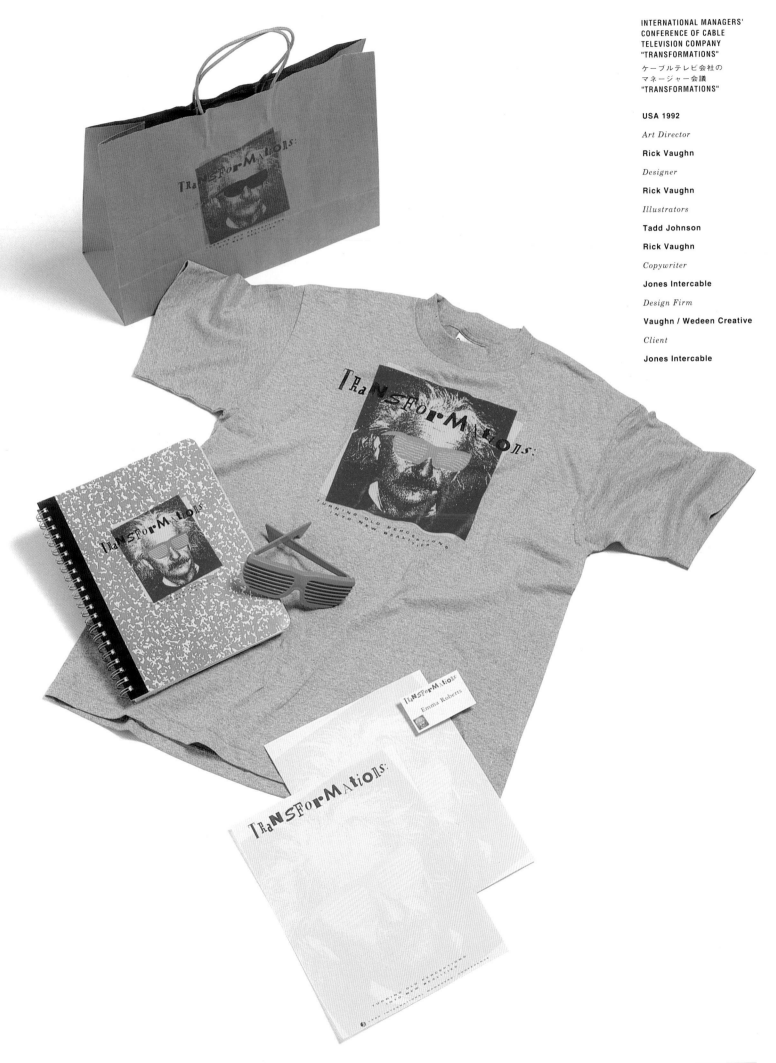

INTERNATIONAL MANAGERS'
CONFERENCE OF CABLE
TELEVISION COMPANY
"TRANSFORMATIONS"
ケーブルテレビ会社の
マネージャー会議
"TRANSFORMATIONS"

USA 1992

Art Director

Rick Vaughn

Designer

Rick Vaughn

Illustrators

Tadd Johnson

Rick Vaughn

Copywriter

Jones Intercable

Design Firm

Vaughn / Wedeen Creative

Client

Jones Intercable

GRAPHIC ARTS MESSAGE '92
グラフィックアーツメッセージ'92

JAPAN 1992

Creative Director

Naomi Enami

Art Director

Neville Brody

Designers

Mariko Yamamoto

Masaki Kimura

Design Firm

Propeller Art Works

Client

Too

TYPESETTING COMPANY'S SEMINAR
"DANCIN' TYPOGRAPHY"
写植会社主催セミナー
"ダンシン　タイポグラフィー"

JAPAN 1988

Art Director

Katsumi Asaba

Designer

Keiko Mineishi

Photographer

Kazumi Kurigami

Artist

Seiko Mikami

Design Firm

Asaba Design

Client

Shaken

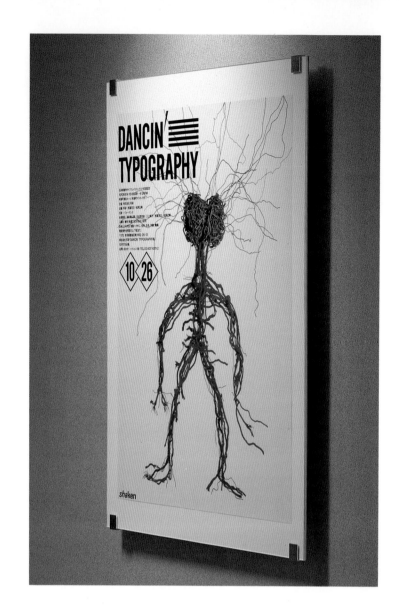

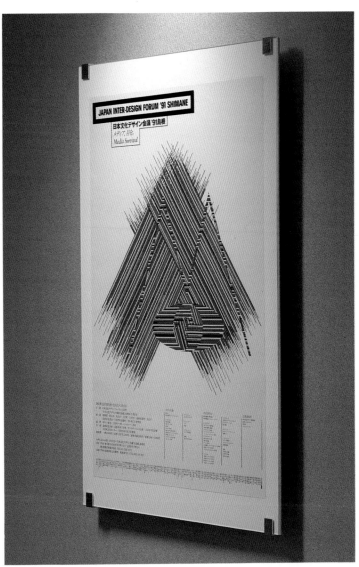

JAPAN INTER-DESIGN FORUM
'91 SIMANE
日本文化デザイン会議 '91島根

JAPAN 1991

Art Director

Katsumi Asaba

Designer

Keiko Mineishi

Copywriter

Katsumi Asaba

Conputer Graphics

Hiroshi Goto

Design Firm

Asaba Design

Client

JIDF

**INTERNATIONAL SYMPOSIUM OF
SERVICE OF CITY GAS
"GEO-CATASTROPHE"**
ガス会社主催の国際シンポジウム
"ジオカタストロフィ"

JAPAN 1991

Creative Director

Takashi Tsumura

Art Director

Masayuki Shimizu

Designers

Masayuki Shimizu

Nio Kimura

Photographer

Katsuzi Nishikawa

Design Firm

Heter-O-Doxy Protprast

Agent

CN

Client

**Research Institute for
Culture, Energy and Life**

4

4

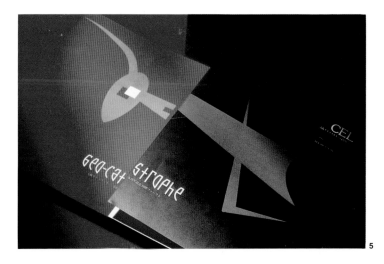

5

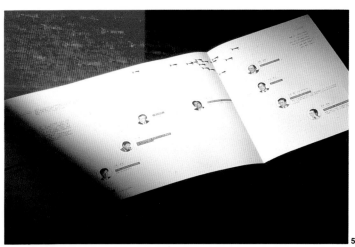

5

Item

1. Poster
2. Judgment panel
3. Envelope & Holder &
   Lead package
4. Brochure
5. Program
6. Ticket holder & Ticket

6

6

DESIGN SEMINAR "JO DUFFY"
デザインセミナー "JO DUFFY"

AUSTRALIA 1992

Art Director

Kevin Wilkins

Designer

Kevin Wilkins

Photographer

Kevin Wilkins

Illustrator

Kevin Wilkins

Copywriter

Kevin Wilkins

Design Firm

Siren

Client

**Spicers Paper /
Hosanne Emery**

**EXHIBITION AND SEMINAR
"COMMUNICATING IDEAS ARTFULLY"**
展示会とセミナー
"COMMUNICATING IDEAS ARTFULLY"

USA 1989

Art Director
Susan Slover

Designer
Cliff Morgan

Photographers
Various

Illustrators
Various

Copywriter
Laura Silverman

Design Firm
Susan Slover Design

Client
Steelcase Design Partnership

CONFERENCE
"PRODUCT SEMANTICS AND
VISUAL SEMOTICS IN DESIGN"

工業美術大学の会議
"PRODUCT SEMANTICS AND
VISUAL SEMOTICS IN DESIGN"

FINLAND 1991

Art Director

Kari Piippo

Designer

Kari Piippo

Illustrator

Kari Piippo

Design Firm

Kari Piippo Oy

Client

**University of
Industrial Arts Helsinki**

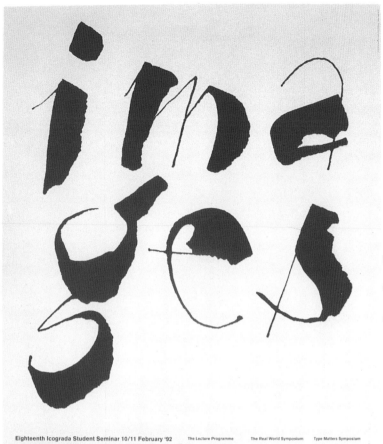

LECTURE "IMAGES"
レクチャー "IMAGES"

UK 1992

Art Director

Alan Fletcher

Designer

Alan Fletcher

Design Firm

Pentagram Design

Client

ICOGRADA (International Council of Graphic and Design Associates)

Eighteenth Icograda Student Seminar 10/11 February '92

The speakers are Malcolm Garrett, Benoît Jacques, Javier Mariscal, Paula Scher, Erik Spiekermann and Michael Wolff.

The Icograda Student Seminars have annually attracted some 1200 design students from all over Europe. They are the most important international gathering of students and their lecturers. This year the programme has additional speakers and events. It is also open to practising designers for the first time.

icograda International Council of Graphic Design Associations

The Lecture Programme

9.15 am to 12.00. 10 & 11 February
The theme of the speakers will be
on the design process, commencing
with initial ideas through to the
final solution.

Chairman: Alan Fletcher (Pentagram)

The Odeon Cinema
Marble Arch, London W1

Monday 10 February

Malcolm Garrett UK
Benoît Jacques Belgium
Paula Scher USA

Tuesday 11 February

Javier Mariscal Spain
Michael Wolff UK
Erik Spiekermann Germany

The Real World Symposium

2.30 pm to 5.00. Monday 10 February
Discussion workshops on the realities
of earning a living. Held by practising
designers for the seminar delegates.

Chairman: Chris Ludlow (CSD)

Chartered Society of Designers
29 Bedford Square, London WC1

The Henrion Evening

6.30 pm to 8.30. Monday 10 February
Additional ticket required. An informal
gathering to meet the speakers and
other delegates.

Chairman: Mary Mullin (Icograda)

Pentagram
11 Needham Road
London W11 .

Type Matters Symposium

2.30 pm to 5.00. Tuesday 11 February
Discussion workshops on the state
of the art. Held by practising designers
and typographers for the seminar
delegates.

Chairman: Colin Banks (STD)

Society of Typographic Designers
29 Bedford Square, London WC1

For information contact:

David Campbell (Organiser)

Icograda Student Seminars
Banks Sadler Ltd
15 Pratt Mews London NW1
Telephone: (071) 388 9000
Fax: (071) 383 4794

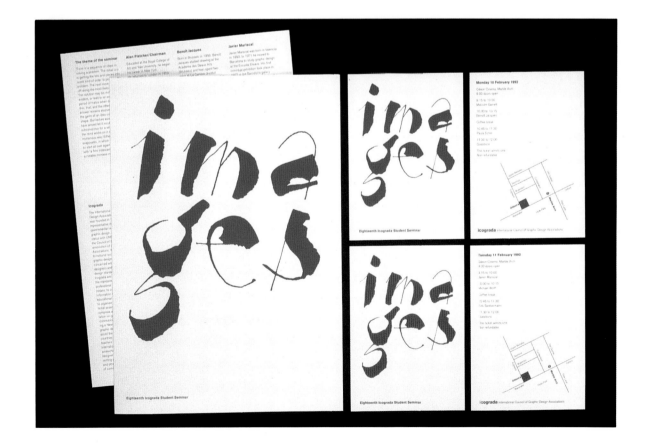

ICLA '91 TOKYO
第13回国際比較文学会東京会議

JAPAN 1991

Art Director

Masaaki Hiromura

Designers

Masaaki Hiromura

Takafumi Kusagaya

Design Firm

Hiromura Design Office

Planner

Seigo Kaneko

Client

**The ICLA '91 Congress
Executive Committee**

P.31
ECO DESIGN FORUM
エコ・デザインフォーラム

JAPAN 1990

Art Director

Kenzo Kobayashi

Designers

Kenzo Kobayashi

Hideo Ogino

Copywriter

Kenzo Kobayashi

Design Firm

Kenzo Kobayashi Design

Client

Tokyo Design Network

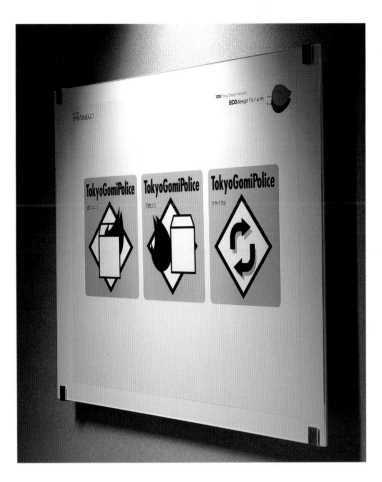

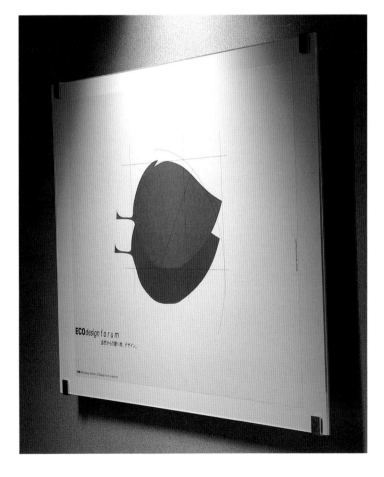

**LECTURE SERIES
"ART AND ARCHITECTURE"**

講演シリーズ
"ART AND ARCHITECTURE"

UK 1991

Art Director

John Rushworth

Designers

John Rushworth

Vince Frost

Design Firm

Pentagram Design

Client

Art and Architecture

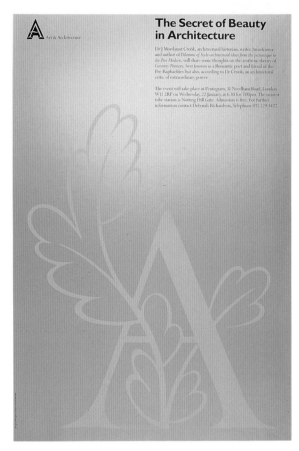

THE COMPUTER GRAPHIC
DESIGN EVENT
"3 TUESDAYS"
コンピューター グラフィック
デザイン イベント
"3 TUESDAYS"

USA 1991

Art Director

Doug Akagi

Designer

Doug Akagi

Illustrator

Dorothy Remington

Copywriters

Chuck Byrne

Elizabeth Byrne

Design Firm

Akagi Design

Client

AIGA

LECTURE "AMBASZ"
レクチャー "AMBASZ"

UK 1992

Art Director

Alan Fletcher

Designer

Alan Fletcher

Design Firm

Pentagram Design

Client

Pentagram / Design Council

LECTURE "BELLINI"
レクチャー "BELLINI"

UK 1991

Art Director

Alan Flotoher

Designers

Alan Fletcher

Eamon Brennan

Design Firm

Pentagram Design

Client

Pentagram / Design Museum

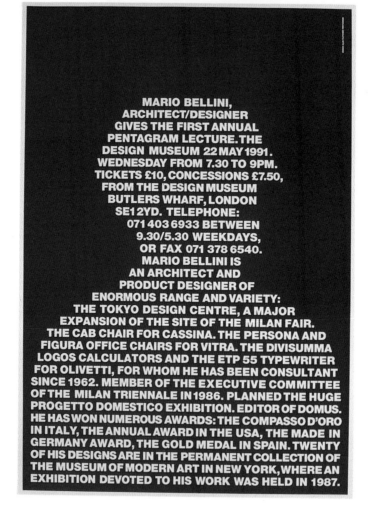

STUDENT SEMINAR "IMAGES"
学生セミナー "IMAGES"

UK 1990

Art Director

Alan Fletcher

Designer

Alan Fletcher

Design Firm

Pentagram Design

Client

ICOGRADA (International Council of Graphic and Design Associates)

images

For information please contact:
Banks Sadler Ltd, 15 Pratt Mews
London NW1 0AD, Tel (071) 388 9101
Telex 261200, Fax (071) 383 4794

Wolfgang Weingart (Swi) on typography
Peter Brookes (UK) on illustration
Henry Steiner (Hong Kong) on symbols
Martin Pedersen (USA) on magazines

Theme of the seminar:
The design process
from the idea to
the final solution

Seventeenth Icograda Student Seminar
9:30am to 12:00 on 11/12 February 1991
Odeon Cinema, Marble Arch, London
International Council of Graphic Design Associations

Design Alan Fletcher/Pentagram

TOKYO CREATIVE '91
東京クリエイティブ'91

JAPAN 1991

Art Director

Shinsuke Mochida

Designer

Shinsuke Mochida

Copywriter

Michiaki Taguchi

Design Firm

Sindbad Design

Client

Tokyo Creative

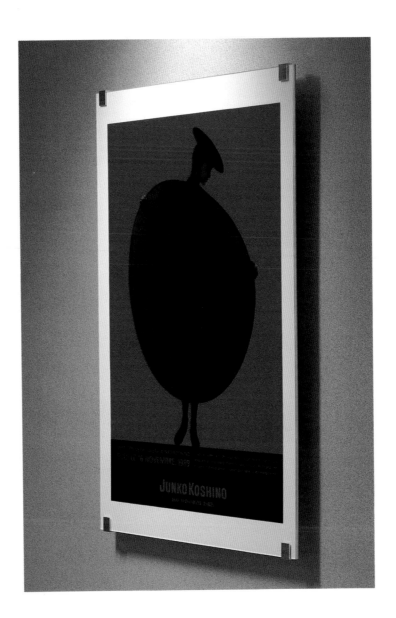

JUNKO KOSHINO 10AV.MONTAIGNE
コシノ ジュンコ 10AV.MONTAIGNE

JAPAN 1989

Art Director
Katsuhiro Kinoshita

Designer
Katsuhiro Kinoshita

Photographers
Shigeyuki Morishita

Ko Saito

Design Firm
Design Club

Client
Junko Koshino Design Office

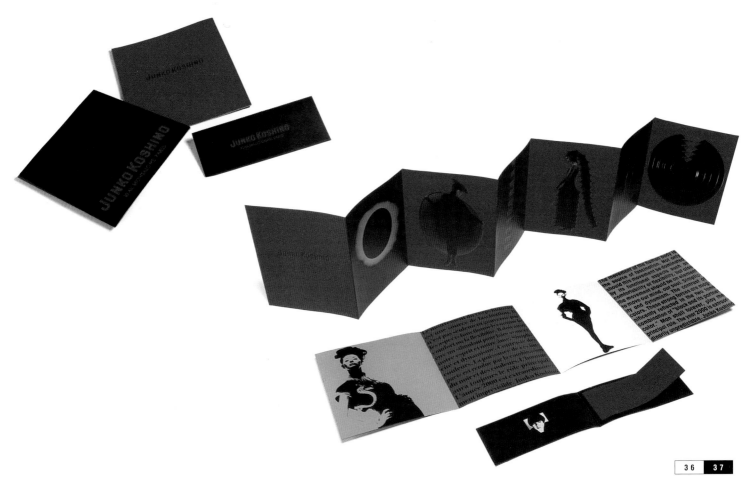

P.38
91-'92 FALL + WINTER
PARIS COLLECTION
'91-'92 秋冬パリコレクション

JAPAN 1990

Art Director

Hisao Sugiura

Designers

Hisao Sugiura

Toshio Matsuura

Illustrator

Minako Saito

Design Firm

Studio Super Compass

Client

Yohji Yamamoto

FASHION COLLECTION
"NUNO GAMA"
ファッションコレクション
"NUNO GAMA"

PORTUGAL 1991

Art Director

Antero Ferreira

Designers

Antero Ferreira

Costanza Puglisi

Photographer

Oscar Almeida

Design Firm

Antero Ferreira Design

Client

Nuno Gama Textil

SORORITY RUSH AT
DRAKE UNIVERSITY
"WE'VE GOT THE BEAT"
ドレイク大学友愛会の
加入勧誘プロモーション
"WE'VE GOT THE BEAT"

USA 1990

Art Director

John Sayles

Designer

John Sayles

Illustrator

John Sayles

Copywriter

Wendy Lyons

Design Firm

Sayles Graphic Design

Client

Drake University

COLLEGE EVENT
"BUILDING BLOCKS FOR SUCCESS"
大学イベント
"BUILDING BLOCKS FOR SUCCESS"

USA 1991

Art Director

John Sayles

Designer

John Sayles

Illustrator

John Sayles

Copywriter

Wendy Lyons

Design Firm

Sayles Graphic Design

Client

Northwestern University

BACK-TO SCHOOL CAMPAIGN
新学期キャンペーン

USA 1990

Art Directors

Daniel Olson

Charles S. Anderson

Designers

Charles S. Anderson

Daniel Olson

Design Firm

Charles S. Anderson Design

Client

The Bon Marche
Department Stores Seattle, WA

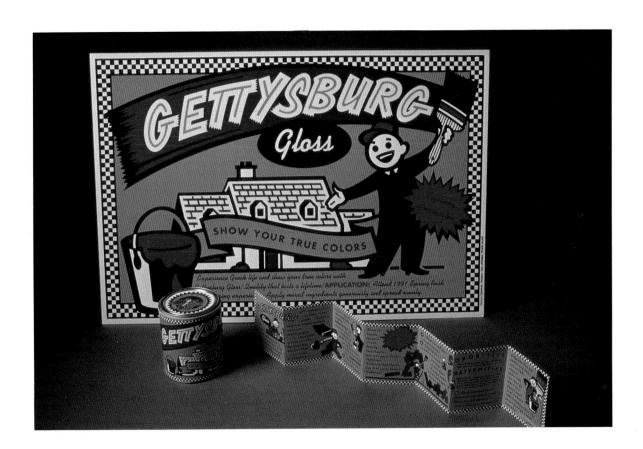

COLLEGE EVENT
"GETTYSBURG GLOSS"
大学イベント
"GETTYSBURG GLOSS"

USA 1990

Art Director

John Sayles

Designer

John Sayles

Copywriter

Wendy Lyons

Design Firm

Sayles Graphic Design

Client

Gettysburg College

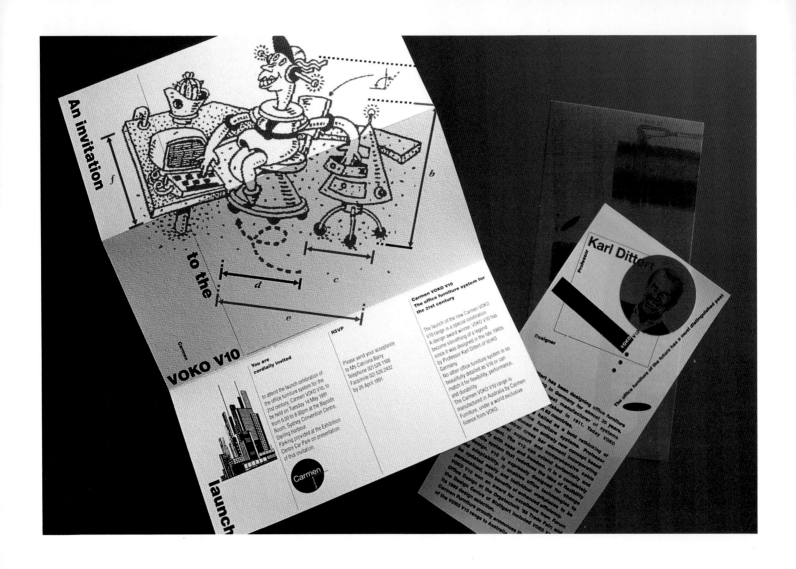

PROMOTION OF A NEW LINE OF
FURNITURE "VOKO 10"
家具の新ラインアップ発売
プロモーション
"VOKO 10"

AUSTRALIA 1991

Creative Director

Garry Emery

Art Director

Emery Vincent Associates

Designer

Emery Vincent Associates

Photographer

John Gollings

Illustrator

Emery Vincent Associates

Copywriter

Jackie Cooper

Design Firm

Emery Vincent Associates

Client

Carmen Furniture (sales)

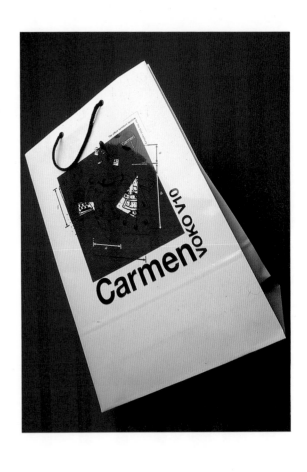

**END OF SEASON SALE OF
FURNITURE & ACCESSORIES
BOUTIQUE**

家具とアクセサリー店の
シーズン末セール

SWITZERLAND 1987-1992

Art Director

Michael Baviera

Design Firm

BBV

Client

Rita Hess, Thalwil

**END OF SEASON SALEOF
FASHION BOUTIQUE**

ファッションブティックの
シーズン末セール

SWITZERLAND 1988-1992

Art Director

Michael Baviera

Design Firm

BBV

Client

Wohnflex, Zürich

YOHJI YAMAMOTO FEMME
PARIS COLLECTION
ヨージ ヤマモト フェム
パリ コレクション

JAPAN 1990
Art Director
Hisao Sugiura
Designers
Hisao Sugiura
Toshio Matsuura
Design Firm
Studio Super Compass
Client
Yohji Yamamoto

**NEW BRAND EXHIBITION
"IM THE SHIRT WOMENS"**
新ブランドデビュー展示会
"アイム ザ・シャツ ウイメンズ"

JAPAN 1992

Art Director

Shuji Kajiwara

Designer

Shuji Kajiwara

Photographer

Sadafusa Furukawa

Copywriter

Masayuki Minoda

Design Firm

D-Planet

Client

Hamilton

PREVIEW EVENT
"LIFETIME TELEVISION"
予告イベント
"LIFETIME TELEVISION"

USA 1992

Creative Director

Gail Rigelhaupt

Designer

Gail Rigelhaupt

Photographer

Peggy Sirota

Copywriter

Jayne Tsuchiyama

Design Firm

Rigelhaupt Design

Client

Lifetime Television

ARFLEX EXECUTIVE COLLECTION
アルフレックス エグゼクティブ
コレクション

JAPAN 1988

Art Director

Shinji Hinode

Designer

Shinji Hinode

Photographer

ZOOM

Interior Cordinator

Fujiko Nemoto

Design Firm

APO

Client

Arflex Japan

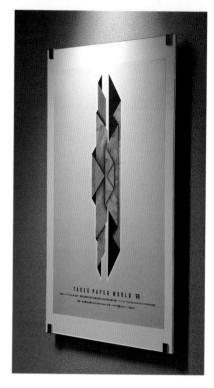

PAPER DISTRIBUTOR'S SHOW
"TAKEO PAPER WORLD '90"

紙卸売商のショー
"竹尾ペーパーワールド'90"

JAPAN 1990

Art Director

Kenya Hara

Designer

Kenya Hara

Design Firm

Nippon Design Center

Client

Takeo

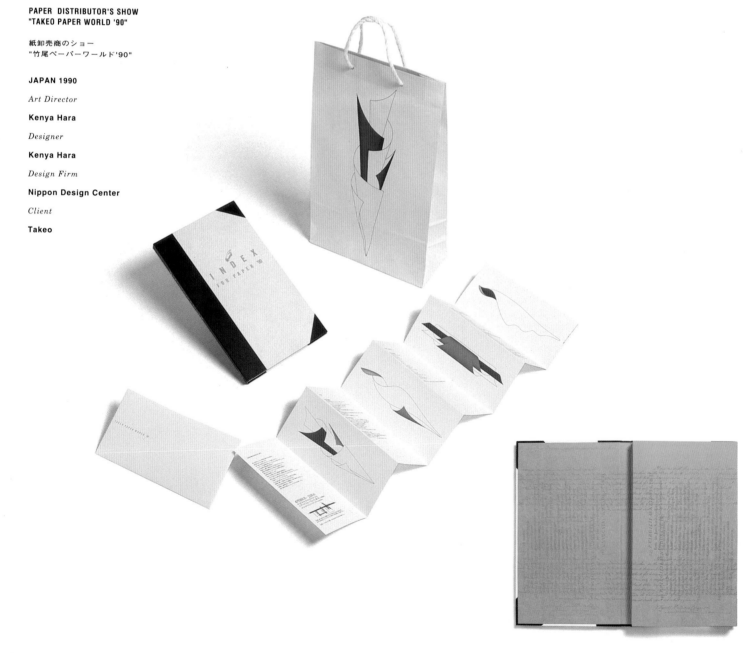

PAPER DISTRIBUTOR'S SHOW
"TAKEO PAPER WORLD '91"

紙卸売商のショー
"竹尾ペーパーワールド'91"

JAPAN 1991

Art Director

Kenya Hara

Designer

Kenya Hara

Design Firm

Nippon Design Center

Client

Takeo

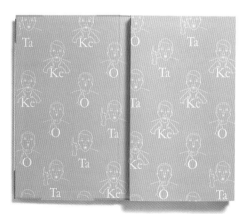

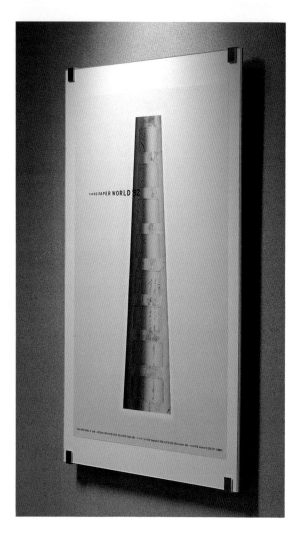

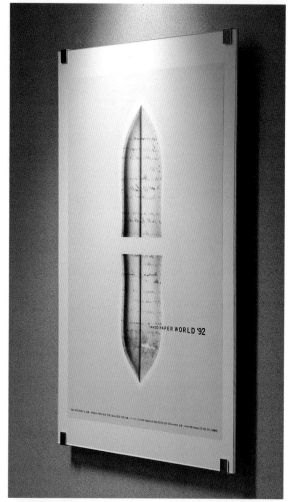

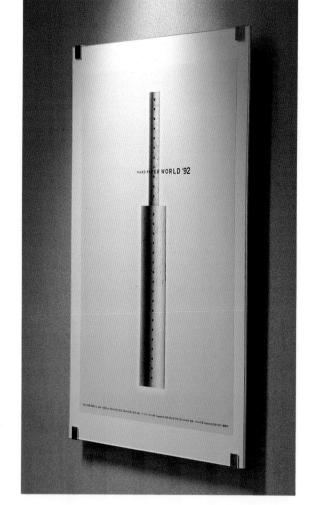

**PAPER DISTRIBUTOR'S SHOW
"TAKEO PAPER WORLD '92"**

紙卸売商のショー
"竹尾ペーパーワールド'92"

JAPAN 1992

Art Director

Kenya Hara

Designer

Kenya Hara

Design Firm

Nippon Design Center

Client

Takeo

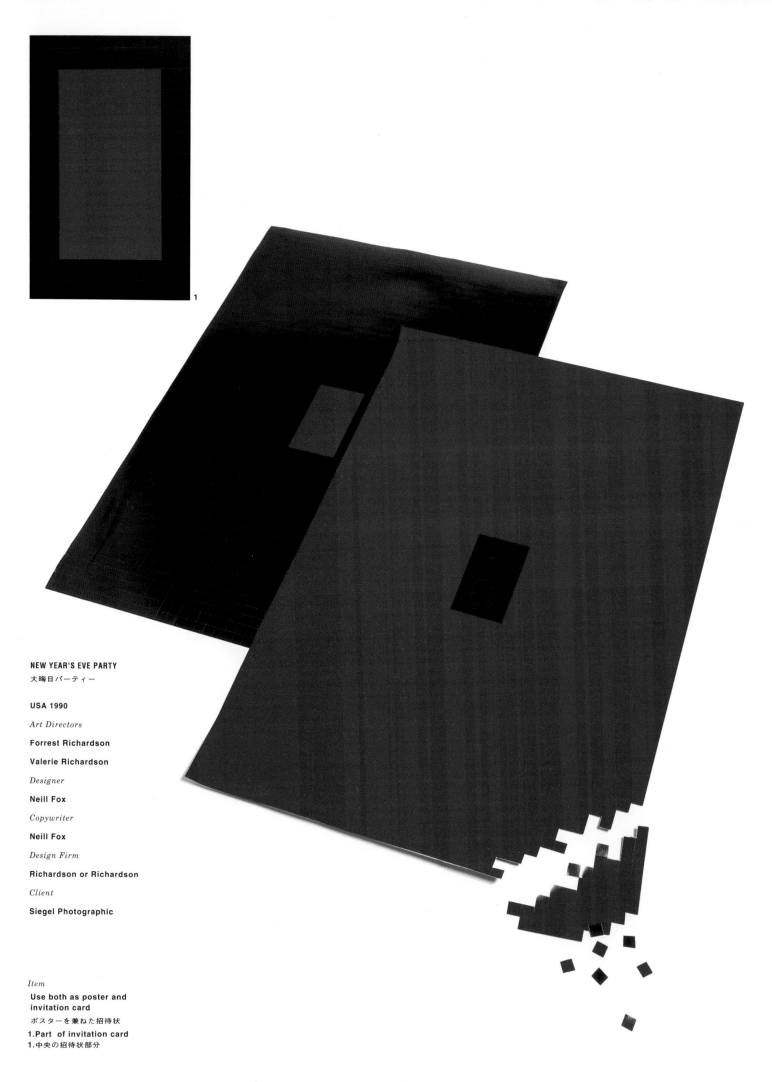

NEW YEAR'S EVE PARTY
大晦日パーティー

USA 1990

Art Directors

Forrest Richardson

Valerie Richardson

Designer

Neill Fox

Copywriter

Neill Fox

Design Firm

Richardson or Richardson

Client

Siegel Photographic

Item

Use both as poster and
invitation card
ポスターを兼ねた招待状
1.Part of invitation card
1.中央の招待状部分

TEA CEREMONY PARTY "SABIE"
茶美会・然

JAPAN 1991
Art Director
Koichi Sato
Designer
Koichi Sato
Client
Sabie

**1991 CYSTIC FIBROSIS
CELEBRITY EVENT**
会社の記念イベント
CYSTIC FIBROSIS 1991

USA 1991

Art Director

Steve Wedeen

Designer

Steve Wedeen

Illustrator

Steve Wedeen

Copywriter

Cystic Fibrosis

Design Firm

Vaughn / Wedeen Creative

Client

Cystic Fibrosis

**TEN YEARS IN THE MAKING
ANNIVERSARY "SAVE THE DATE"**
制作活動10周年記念イベント
"SAVE THE DATE"

USA 1992

Art Director

Jack Anderson

Designers

Jack Anderson

Jani Drewfs

Illustrators

David Bates

Yutaka Sasaki

Copywriter

Pamela Mason-Davey

Design Firm

Horna'l Anderson Design Works

Client

Hornall Anderson Design Works

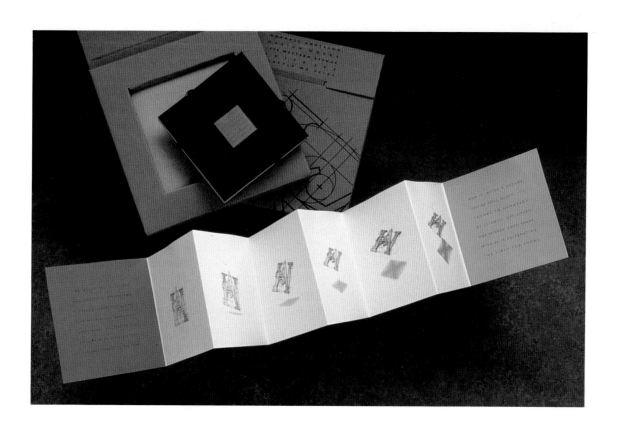

COMPANY EVENT
"PRESIDENTS CLUB CRUISE"
会社のイベント
"PRESIDENTS CLUB CRUISE"

USA 1991

Art Director

John Sayles

Designer

John Sayles

Illustrator

John Sayles

Design Firm

Sayles Graphic Design

Client

National Travelers Life

FORMAL DINNER
"WE'RE SAVING A PLACE FOR YOU"
フォーマルディナー
"WE'RE SAVING A PLACE FOR YOU"

USA 1990

Art Director

John Sayles

Designer

John Sayles

Illustrator

John Sayles

Copywriter

Mary Riche

Design Firm

Sayles Graphic Design

Client

Palmer Communications

2ND ANNUAL HALLOWEEN PARTY "ZOO BOO TWO"
第2回年次ハロウィンパーティー
"ZOO BOO TWO"

USA 1990

Art Director

Steve Wedeen

Designer

Dan Flynn

Illustrator

Gerhold Smith

Copywriter

Rio Grande Zoo

Design Firm

Vaughn / Wedeen Creative

Client

Rio Grande Zoo

**7th ANNUAL PROMOTION
"RUN FOR THE ZOO"**
**7周年プロモーション
"RUN FOR THE ZOO"**

USA 1992

Art Director

Steve Wedeen

Designer

Steve Wedeen

Illustrator

Kevin Tolman

Design Firm

Vaughn / Wedeen Creative

Client

Dion's Pizza

3RD ANNUAL HALLOWEEN PARTY
"ZOO BOO THREE"
第3回年次ハロウィンパーティー
"ZOO BOO THREE"

USA 1991

Art Director

Steve Wedeen

Designer

Steve Wedeen

Illustrator

Steve Wedeen

Copywriter

Rio Grande Zoo

Design Firm

Vaughn / Wedeen Creative

Client

Rio Grande Zoo

**SACRAMENTO ZOO 65th BIRTHDAY
CELEBRATION**

サクラメント動物園65周年記念
プロモーション

USA 1992

Creative Director

Michael Dunlavey

Designers

Nancy McMurchie

Kevin Yee

Illustrator

Dave Stevenson

Design Firm

The Dunlavey Studio

Client

Sacramento Zoological Society

**OPEN HOUSE OF
ARCHITECTURE DESIGN OFFICE**
建築デザイン事務所の
オープンハウスパーティー

USA 1990

Creative Director

Kerry Burg

Art Director

Klindt Parker

Designer

Klindt Parker

Illuatrator

Klindt Parker

Copywriter

Jerilyn Warren

Design Firm

NBBJ-Graphic Design

Client

NBBJ-Tuscon

Item
Invitation set
招待状のセット
1. **Invitation card**
2. **Name tag**
3. **Confetti**

**OPEN HOUSE AT A HIGH SCHOOL
"CHART YOUR COURSE"**
高校でのオープンハウスイベント
"CHART YOUR COURSE"

USA 1991

Art Director

John Sayles

Designer

John Sayles

Illustrator

John Sayles

Copywriter

Carol Mouchka

Design Firm

Sayles Graphic Design

Client

Dowling High School

CELEBRATION EVENT
"GREAT DESIGN TAKES
CENTER STAGE"
作品展示受賞式
"GREAT DESIGN TAKES
CENTER STAGE"

USA 1992

Art Director

John Sayles

Designer

John Sayles

Illustrator

John Sayles

Copywriter

Wendy Lyons

Design Firm

Sayles Graphic Design

Client

James River Paper

THE 33th ANNIVERSARY EVENT
"TOKYO TOWER FANTASTIC 333"
33周年記念イベント
"東京タワーファンタスティック 333"

JAPAN 1991

Creative Director

Toshirou Suzuki

Art Director

Isao Imabayashi

Designers

Megumi Yabuki

Takako Sawada

Toshimitsu Negishi

Copywriter

Chicayoshi Akase

Design Firm

Chocolate

Client

Tokyo Tower

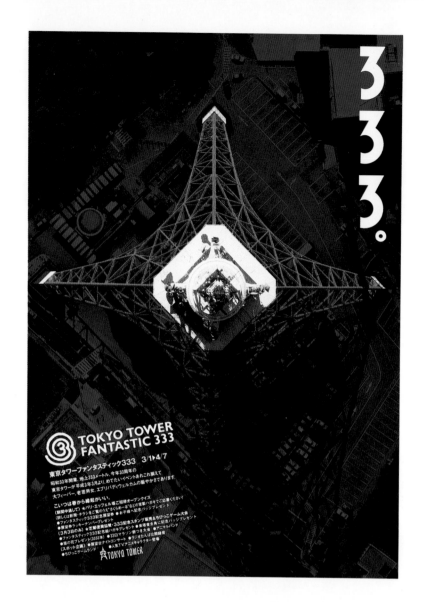

APPRECIATION PARTY FOR
HOSPITAL EMPLOYEES
"SPIN LIKE A TOP"
病院従業員の感謝パーティー
"SPIN LIKE A TOP"

USA 1991

Art Director

Eric Rickabaugh

Designer

Tina Zientarski

Illustrator

Mike Smith

Design Firm

Rickabaugh Graphics

Client

Grant Hospital

Item
1. Invitation card
2. Envelope
3. Raffle ticket
4. Postcard

EVENT "THEATRE 2090"
イベント "THEATRE 2090"

USA 1990

Art Director

Warren Wilkins

Designer

Dan Baker

Illustrator

Dan Baker

Design Firm

Wilkins & Peterson

Client

Seafirst Bank

MTV LAUNCHING PARTY
MTV 始業パーティー

HONG KONG 1991

Art Director

Bethany Bunnell

Designer

Bethany Bunnell

Design Firm

Star TV Creative Services

Client

Star TV

**CELEBRATION OF
THE LAUNCH OF A TV CHANNEL**
テレビ局の開局記念

HONG KONG 1991

Art Directors

Bethany Bunnell

Joe Kurzer

Designer

Catherine Lam

Design Firm

Star TV Creative Services

Client

Star TV

**CELEBRATION OF
THE QUEEN'S 60th BIRTHDAY**
女王陛下の60回目の誕生日イベント

UK 1986

Art Director

Mervyn Kurlansky

Designers

Mervyn Kurlansky

Herman Lelie

Claire Johnson

Illustrator

Wolf Spoerl

Design Firm

Pentagram Design

Client

**The Queen's Birthday
Committee**

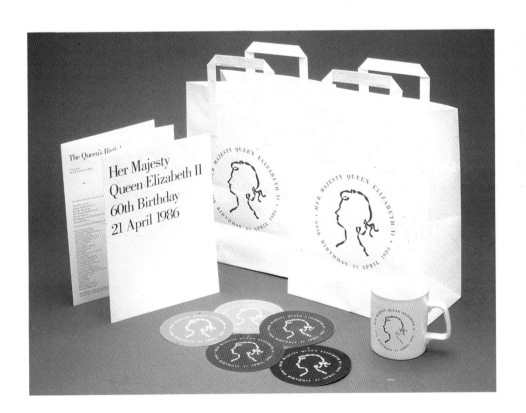

THE GRAND OPENING OF
SHOPPING MALL
"FRANKLIN MILLS"
ショッピングモール
オープニング プロモーション
"FRANKLIN MILLS"

USA 1989

Creative Directors

Fran Albin

Gail Rigelhaupt

Designer

Gail Rigelhaupt

Copywriter

Fran Albin

Design Firm

Rigelhaupt Design

Client

Western Development

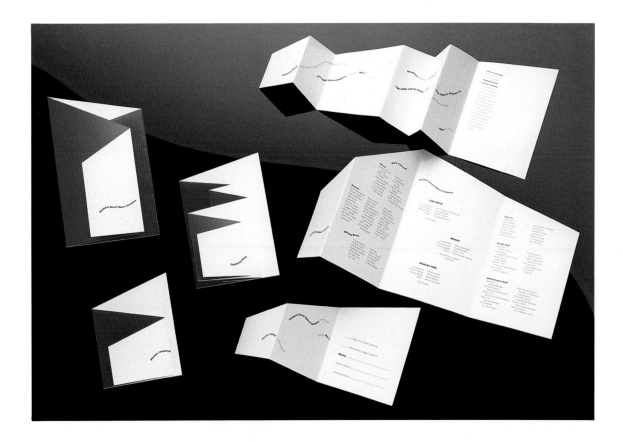

RECEPTION PERTY WITH
DANCE PERFORMANCE
"HUBBARD STREET"
ダンスパフォーマンスと
レセプションパーティ
"HUBBARD STREET"

USA 1989

Art Director

Janis Boehm

Designer

Tracy Gibbons

Design Firm

Janis Boehm Design

Client

Continental Bank

TO PROMOTE THE 500th
ANNIVERSARY OF
THE DISCOVERY OF AMERICA
"1992...AMERICA DISCOVERS
COLUMBUS"
アメリカ大陸発見500周年記念
プロモーション
"1992...AMERICA DISCOVERS
COLUMBUS"

USA 1991

Art Directors

Eric Rickabaugh

Mark Krumel

Designer

Mark Krumel

Illustrators

Anorea Eberbach

Scott Hull Associates

Design Firm

Rickabaugh Graphics

Client

Rickabaugh
Graphics-Designworks

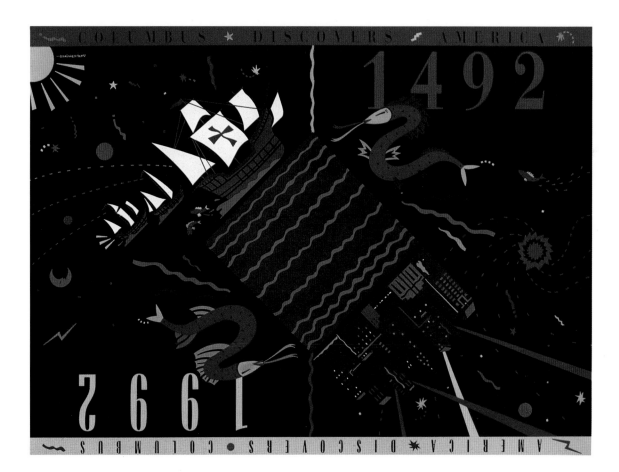

**EVENT "CHRISTMAS CAROLS"
AND PROMOTION "PACIFIC POWER"**
クリスマスイベント
"CHRISTMAS CAROLS"と
プロモーション"PACIFIC POWER"

AUSTRALIA 1991

Art Director

Emery Vincent Associates

Designer

Emery Vincent Associates

Photographer

Emery Vincent Associates

Illustrator

Emery Vincent Associates

Copywriter

Emery Vincent Associates

Design Firm

Emery Vincent Associates

Client

**Pacific power
(New South Wales Electricity)**

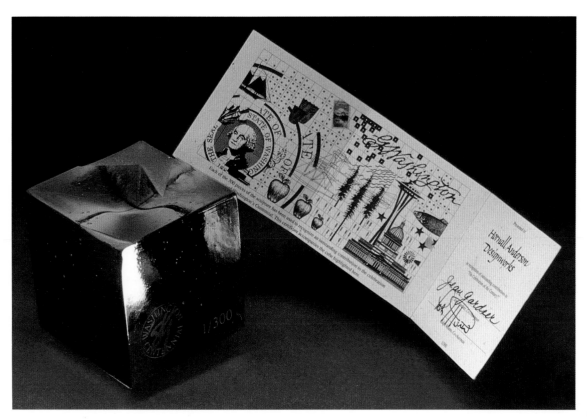

**WASHINGTON STATE CENTENNIAL
AWARDS PROGRAM**
ワシントン州百周年記念賞受賞式

USA 1989

Art Director

Jack Anderson

Designers

Jack Anderson

Mike Courtney

Copywriter

**Washington State Centennial
Commission**

Design Firm

Hornall Anderson Design Works

Client

**Washington State Centennial
Commission**

**WASHINGTON STATE CENTENNIAL
AWARDS PROGRAM**
ワシントン州百周年記念賞受賞式

SEATTLE ART MUSEUM CAMPAIGN
"SAM GOES DOWNTOWN"
シアトル美術館キャンペーン
"SAM GOES DOWNTOWN"

USA 1988

Art Directors

John Hornall

Mike Courtney

Designers

John Hornall

Mike Courtney

Brian O'Neill

David Bates

Design Firm

Hornall Anderson Design Works

Client

Seattle Art Museum

NBBJ CHRISTMAS PARTY
NBBJ クリスマス パーティー

USA 1990

Creative Director
Kerry Burg

Art Director
Margo Sepanski

Designer
Margo Sepanski

Illustrators
Various

Copywriters
Margo Sepanski
Sir Walter Scott (Quote)

Design Firm
NBBJ-Graphic Design

Client
NBBJ-Seattle

**THE AMBIENTE INTERNATIONAL
OPENING PARTY**
アンビエンテ インターナショナル
新社屋竣工記念パーティー

JAPAN 1991

Creative Director

Hiroki Nakagami

Art Director

Hajime Shimizu

Designer

Hiroshi Shoda

Copywriter

Keishi Kitaguchi

Supervisor (diagram)

Yasuyuki Ohhiro

Produce (drawing book)

Molteni & C

Design Firm

Body Plus

Client

Ambiente International

EXHIBITION OPENING PARTY
"EAST MEETS WEST"
展覧会オープニングパーティ
"EAST MEETS WEST"

USA 1989

Creative Directors

Anneke Van Waesburghe

Gail Rigelhaupt

Designer

Gail Rigelhaupt

Design Firm

Rigelhaupt Design

Client

**East Meets West Cultural
International**

OPEN HOUSE PARTY
オープンハウス パーティー

USA 1991

Creative Director

Kerry Burg

Art Director

Doug Keyes

Designer

Doug Keyes

Photographer

Doug Keyes

Copywriter

Doug Keyes

Design Firm

NBBJ - Graphic Design

Client

NBBJ - San Francisco

NBBJ CHRISTMAS PARTY
NBBJ クリスマス パーティー

USA 1991

Creative Director
Kerry Burg

Art Director
Stefanie Choi

Designer
Stefanie Choi

Illustrator
Stefanie Choi

Copywriter
Stefanie Choi

Design Firm
NBBJ - Graphic Design

Client
NBBJ - Seattle

PARTY
"SPANISH SERENADE"
パーティー
"SPANISH SERENADE"

USA 1990

Art Director

Kerry Burg

Designer

Stefanie Choi

Design Firm

NBBJ - Graphic Design

Client

**Music at Kohl Mansion
Auxiliary**

PEÑA · CHAVEZ WEDDING
結婚式 PEÑA & CHAVEZ

USA 1990

Art Director

Marcos Chavez

Designer

Marcos Chavez

Design Firm

Michael Stanard

Client

Marcos and Amairis Chavez

OPENING OF YUFUIN ART MUSEUM
由布院美術館開館プロモーション

JAPAN 1991

Art Director

Tatsuaki Yasuno

Designer

Susumu Utagawa

Photographer

Takayasu Aoki

Design Firm

T.Y.D.

Client

Yufuin Art Museu

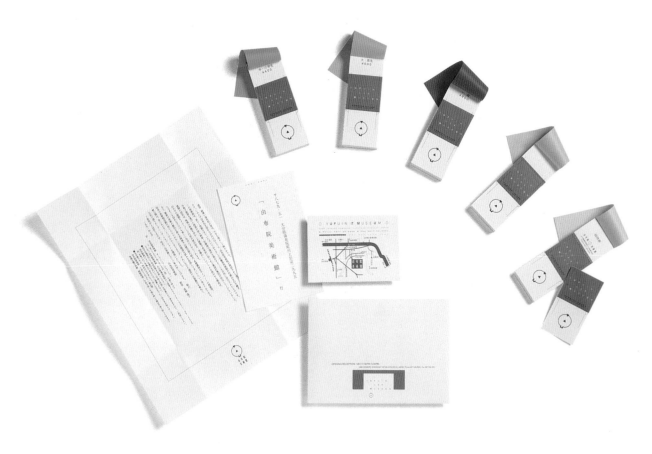

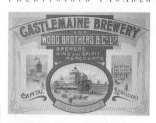

ART EXHIBITION
"REFRESHING!
ART OFF THE PUB WALL"
美術展
"REFRESHING!
ART OFF THE PUB WALL"

AUSTRALIA 1990

Art Director

Colin Rowan

Designer

Colin Rowan

Photographer

Andrew Frollows

Illustrator

Henry Rousel

Copywriters

John O'Brian

Susan Charlton

Design Firm

Powerhouse Museum
Graphic Services

Client

Powerhouse Museum

ART EXHIBITION "ARTFAIR"
美術展 "ARTFAIR"

USA 1992

Art Director

Tommer Peterson

Designer

Tommer Peterson

Copywriter

Tommer Peterson

Design Firm

Wilkins & Peterson

Client

Artfair

THE MONTH'S EVENTS IN A MUSEUM
"ACTION PACKED"
博物館の月間イベント
"ACTION PACKED"

AUSTRALIA 1992

Art Director

Colin Rowan

Designer

Lucy Culliton

Photographer

Andrew Frollows

Copywriters

Colin Rowan

Laurie Figg

Susan Charlton

Design Firm

**Powerhouse Museum
Graphic Services**

Client

Powerhouse Museum

EXHIBITION
"BUSH TOYS AND FURNITURE"
展示会
"BUSH TOYS AND FURNITURE"

AUSTRALIA 1990

Art Director

Colin Rowan

Designers

Colin Rowan

Jason M Cdonald

Photographers

Penelope Clay

Jane Townbend

Illustrator

Colin Rowan

Copywriters

Ann Stepen

David Dolan

Anne Watson

Design Firm

**Powerhouse Museum
Graphic Services**

Client

Powerhouse Museum

STORE WINDOW DISPLAY SHOW
"NEVER DONE"
店頭ウィンドウディスプレイショウ
"NEVER DONE"

AUSTRALIA 1992

Creative Director

Parish Stapleton

Art Director

Colin Rowan

Photographer

David Jones Photography

Copywriters

Ann Stephen

Kimberley Webber

Design Firm

**Powerhouse Museum
Graphic Services**

Client

David Jones

**AIGA COMMUNICATION
GRAPHICS SHOW**
AIGA 通信グラフィックスショー

USA 1991

Art Director

Michael Stanard

Designer

Marcos Chauez

Design Firm

Michael Stanard

Client

AIGA
**(The American Institute of
Graphic Arts)**

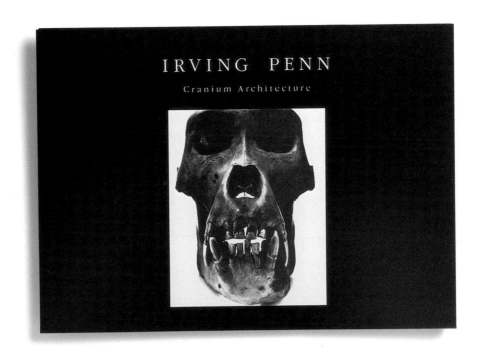

IRVING PENN
"CRANIUM ARCHITECTURE"
アービング・ペン写真展
"頭骨の建築"

JAPAN 1990
Creative Director
Toshihiko Takemura
Art Director
Masanori Uchida
Designer
Masanori Uchida
Client
Gallery・COA

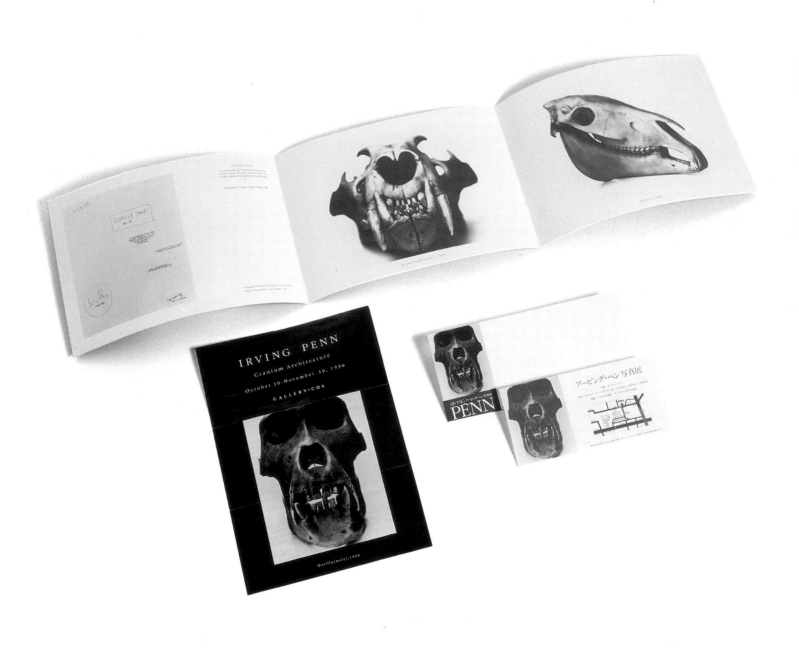

CRAFTS COUNCIL CAMPAIGN
工芸委員会キャンペーン

UK 1991

Art Director

John Rushworth

Designers

John Rushworth

Vince Frost

Design Firm

Pentagram Design

Client

Crafts Council

EXHIBITION
"THE ANTIPODEAN WHEEL"
展示会
"THE ANTIPODEAN WHEEL"

AUSTRALIA 1991

Art Director

Micheal Trudgeon

Designer

Micheal Trudgeon

Design Firm

Crowd Productions

Client

Meat Market Craft Centre

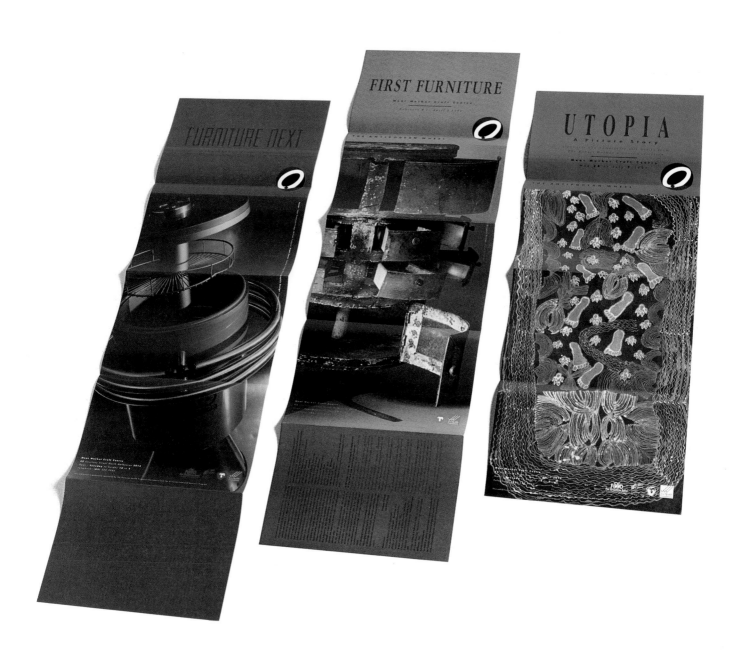

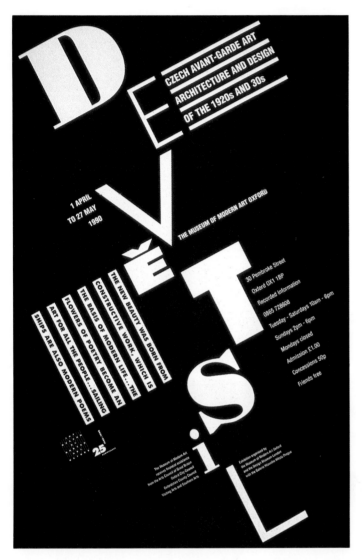

EXHIBITION OF
ART ARCHITECTURE AND DESIGN
"DEVETSIL"
美術建築およびデザイン展示会
"DEVETSIL"

UK 1990

Art Director

Mervyn Kurlansky

Designer

Mervyn Kurlansky

Design Firm

Pentagram Design

Client

Museum of Modern Art

ART EXHIBITION "MAKONDE"
美術展 "MAKONDE"

UK 1989

Art Director

Mervyn Kurlansky

Designer

Mervyn Kurlansky

Design Firm

Pentagram Design

Client

Museum of Modern Art

ART EXHIBITION
"ART FROM SOUTH AFRICA"
美術展
"ART FROM SOUTH AFRICA"

UK 1990

Art Director

Mervyn Kurlansky

Designer

Mervyn Kurlansky

Design Firm

Pentagram Design

Client

Museum of Modern Art

EXHIBITION
"JULISTEMUSEO 1975-1990"
展覧会
"JULISTEMUSEO 1975-1990"

FINLAND 1990

Art Director

Kari Piippo

Designer

Kari Piippo

Illustrator

Kari Piippo

Design Firm

Kari Piippo Oy

Client

Lahti Poster Museum

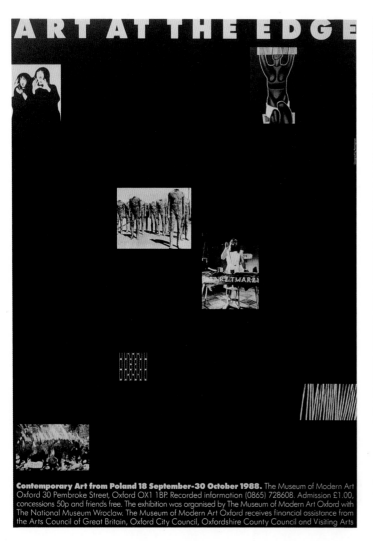

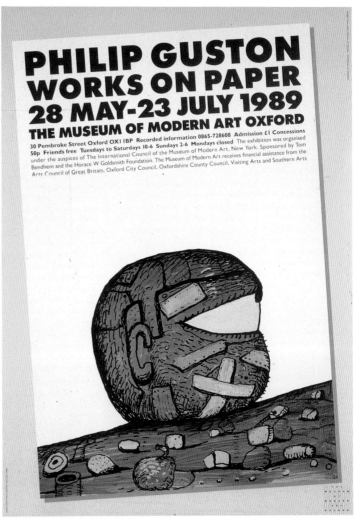

ART EXHIBITION
"ART AT THE EDGE"
美術展
"ART AT THE EDGE"

UK 1987

Art Director

Mervyn Kurlansky

Designers

Mervyn Kurlansky

Robert Dunnet

Design Firm

Pentagram Design

Client

Museum of Modern Art

ART EXHIBITION
"PHILIP GUSTON"
美術展
"PHILIP GUSTON"

UK 1989

Art Director

Mervyn Kurlansky

Designer

Mervyn Kurlansky

Design Firm

Pentagram Design

Client

Museum of Modern Art

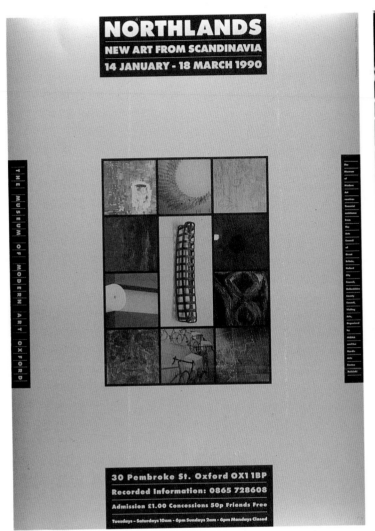

ART EXHIBITION
"NORTHLANDS"
美術展
"NORTHLANDS"

UK 1990

Art Director

Mervyn Kurlansky

Designer

Mervyn Kurlansky

Design Firm

Pentagram Design

Client

Museum of Modern Art

ART EXHIBITION
"SOUR BURNING FLASHERS"
美術展
"SOUR BURNING FLASHERS"

UK 1989

Art Director

Mervyn Kurlansky

Designers

Mervyn Kurlansky

Robert Dunnet

Design Firm

Pentagram Design

Client

Museum of Modern Art

PHOTOGRAPHS, KIMURA IHEE
木村伊兵衛の世界

JAPAN 1992

Designer

Toshio Shiratani

Photographer

Shinji Murakami

Design Firm

Nomade

Client

**Tokyo Metropolitan Museum
of Photography**

P.98
KIYOSHI HASEGAWA EXHIBITION
"長谷川 潔の世界" 展

JAPAN 1991

Creative Director

Nobuo Nakagaki

Art Director

Takashi Shimada

Designer

Takashi Shimada

Design Firm

Nakagaki Design Office

Client

Yokohama Museum of Art

ISAMU NOGUCHI
RETROSPECTIVE 1992
イサム・ノグチ展

JAPAN 1992

Art Director

Kiyoshi Asai

Designers

Kiyoshi Asai

Toshiyuki Bamen

Photographer

Shigeo Anzai

Clients

**The National Museum of
Modern Art, Tokyo**

Imex

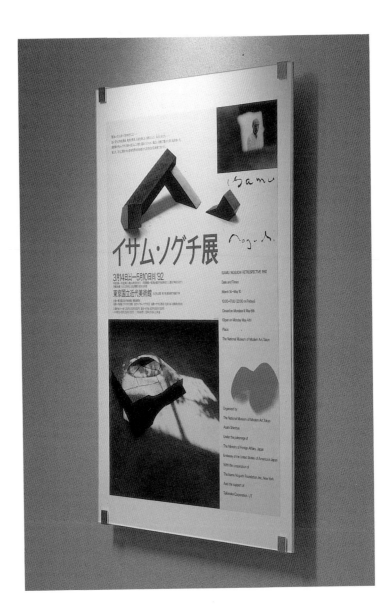

EXHIBITION
"VASES BOXES TRAYS CONTAINERS
FOR IKEBANA"
花の器展

JAPAN 1991

Art Director

Koichi Sato

Designer

Koichi Sato

Client

The Sogetsu Art Museum

MACHIKO OGAWA
CERAMIC EXHIBITION
小川待子展

JAPAN 1990

Art Director

Koichi Sato

Designer

Koichi Sato

Client

The Sogetsu Art Museum

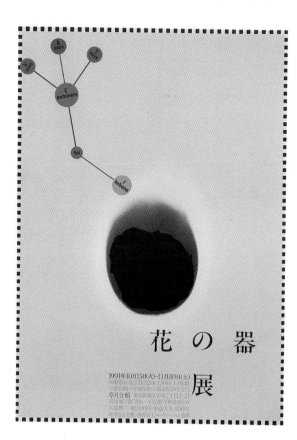

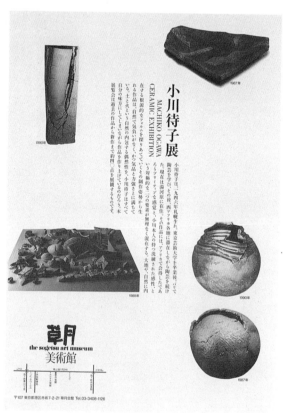

TERRAKADO TAKAYUKI EXHIBITION
"SILICONE MODE GRAPHICS 2"
寺門孝之展
"シリコンモード グラフィックス 2"

JAPAN 1991

Art Director

Takashi Ohta

Photographer

Atsuhiro Kanazawa

Illustrator

Takayuki Terrakado

Copywriter

Takeo Matsuda

Client

Hypercritical

23th APA
第23回 APA 展

JAPAN 1990

Art Director

Keisuke Nagatomo

Designer

Takashi Nomura

Photographer

Shuhei Fukuda

Design Firm

K-Two

Client

APA

HONG KONG ARTISTS'
GUILD ANNOUNCEMENT
"ARTIST OF THE YEAR AWARDS 1991"
香港芸術家協会
"ARTIST OF THE YEAR AWARDS 1991"

HONG KONG 1991

Art Director

Kan Tai-Keung

Designer

Kan Tai-Keung

Design Firm

**Kan Tai-Keung
Design & Associates**

Client

Hong Kong Artists' Guild

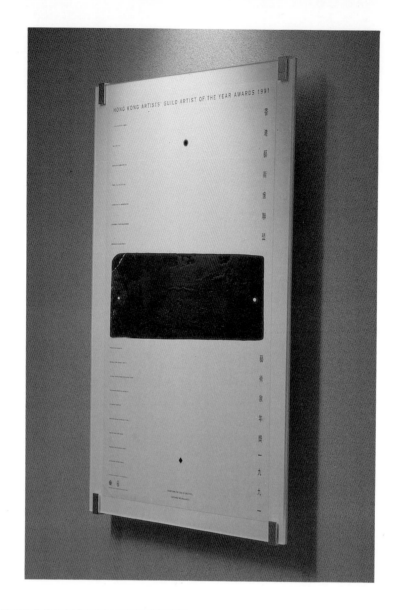

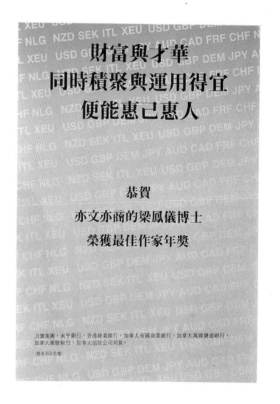

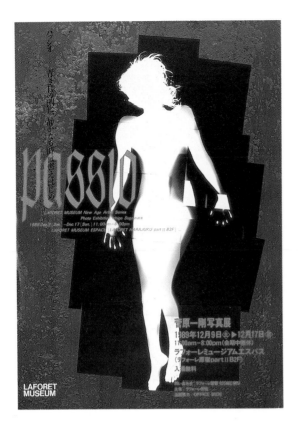

PHOTO EXHIBITION
ICHIGO SUGAWARA "PASSIO"
菅原一剛写真展 "PASSIO"

JAPAN 1989

Art Director
Keishin Nakaseko

Designer
Keishin Nakaseko

Photographer
Ichigo Sugawara

Copywriter
Hironori Okubo

Client
Laforet Harajuku

BRUCE WILLIAMS PHOTO EXHIBITION
ブルース・ウィリアムズ写真展
"死ぬにはいい日だ"

JAPAN 1990

Art Director
Akira Kuriyama

Designer
Kurumi Miura

Photographer
Bruce Williams

Copywriter
Akira Kuriyama

Client
Laforet Harajuku

"LAJOS KASSÁK" EXHIBITION
カシャーク全貌展

JAPAN 1991

Art Director

Kenzo Izutani

Designers

Kenzo Izutani

Aki Hirai

Illustrator

Lajos Kassák

Design Firm

Kenzo Izutani Office

Client

Parco

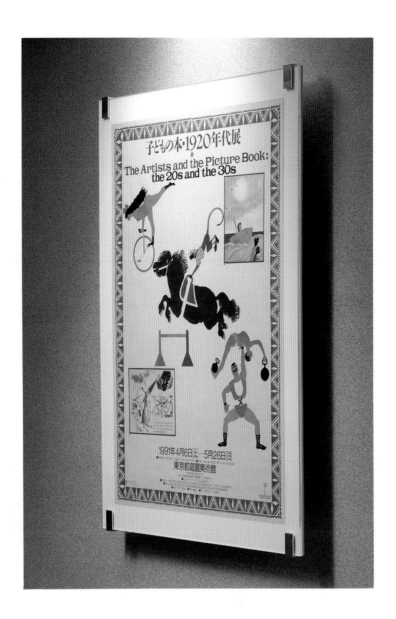

EXHIBITION OF THE ARTIST AND
THE PICTURE BOOK
THE TWENTIES ON THE THIRTIES
子どもの本・1920年代展

JAPAN 1991

Art Director

Nobuo Nakagaki

Designers

Nobuo Nakagaki

Hiromi Watanabe

Design Firm

Nakagaki Design Office

Client

Tokyo Metropolitan Teien
Art Museum

ART EXHIBITION
"ERIC FRASER"
美術展
"ERIC FRASER"

UK 1991

Creative Director

Geoff Aldridge

Art Director

Sally Mcintosh

Designers

Paula Peachey

Sally Mcintosh

Clare Harris

Photographer

Nicholas Gentilli

Illustrator

Eric Fraser

Copywriter

Patricia Hodgson

Exhibition Director

Richard Greenwood

Design Firm

Communication by Design

Client

British Gas

EXHIBITION
"CARRIED AWAY"
展示会
"CARRIED AWAY"

AUSTRALIA 1988

Art Director

Colin Rowan

Designers

Colin Rowan

Romaine Joseph

Photographer

Andrew Frollows

Copywriter

Warren Wickman

Design Firm

Powerhouse Museum
Graphic Services

Client

Powerhouse Museum

EXHIBITION
"JEAN - PIERRE RAYNAUD"
"ジャン=ピエール・レイノー" 展

JAPAN 1992

Art Director

Katsumi Asaba

Designer

Keiko Mineishi

Photographer

Tsuyoshi Saito

Copywriter

Katsumi Asaba

Artist

Jean - Pierre Raynaud

Design Firm

Asaba Design

Client

Art Tower Mito

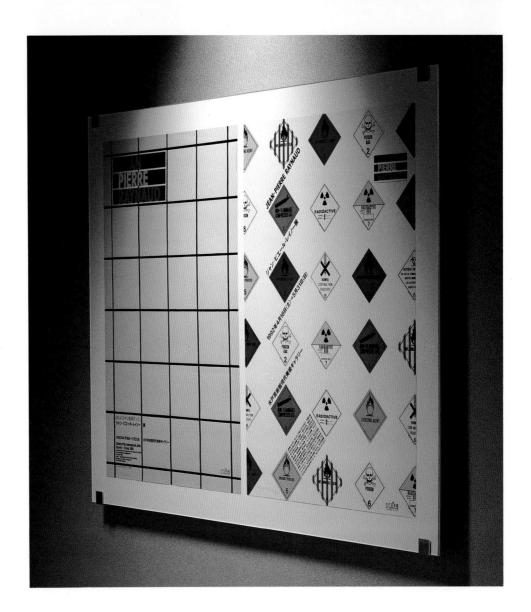

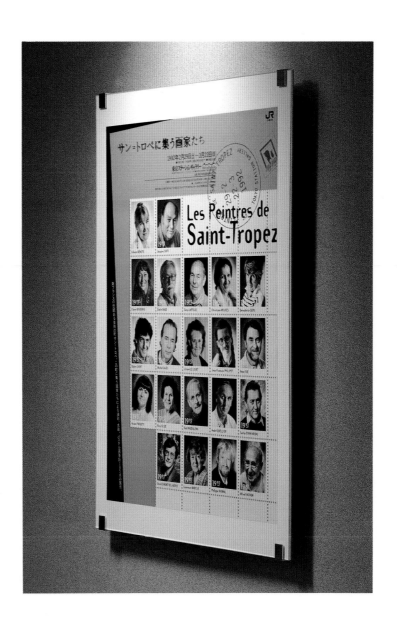

LES PEINTRES DE SAINT-TROPEZ
サン゠トロペに集う画家たち

JAPAN 1992

Art Director

Tatsuaki Yasuno

Designers

Susumu Utagawa

Masakatsu Oikawa

Akira Kikuchi

Design Firm

T.Y.D.

Client

Tokyo Station Gallery

THE WORLD OF BOX
箱の世界

JAPAN 1991

Art Director

Katsumi Asaba

Designer

Keiko Mineishi

Photographer

Tsuyoshi Saito

Design Firm

Asaba Design

Client

Art Tower Mito

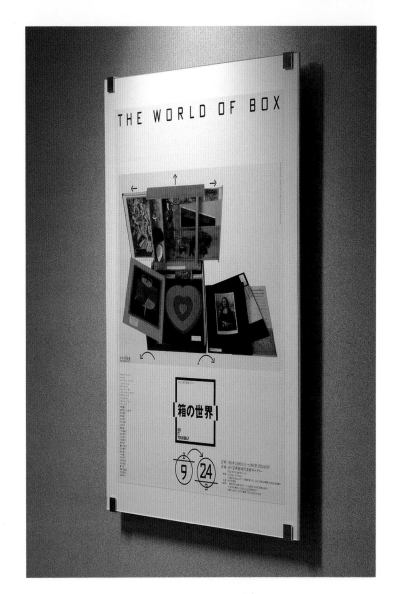

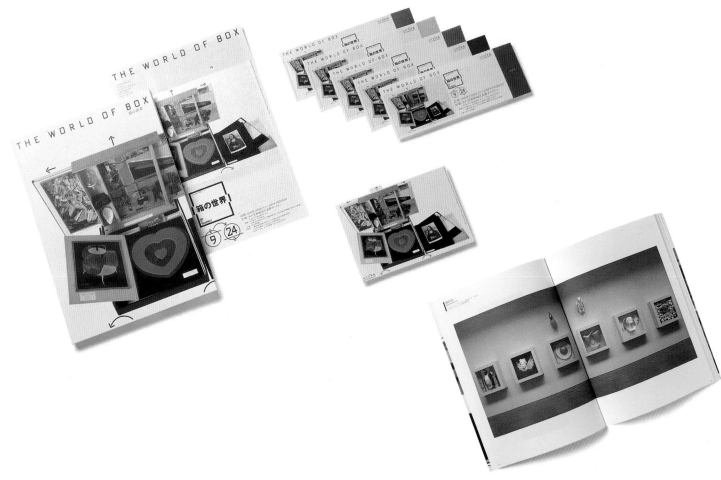

GENKOYOSHI EXHIBITION
原稿用紙展

JAPAN 1989

Creative Director

Seiji Koseki

Art Director

Tatsuomi Majima

Designer

Tatsuomi Majima

Artists

Tatsuomi Majima

Masao Yamamoto

Michiko Yano

Saburo Ota

Noriko Kurezumi

Shigesato Itoi

Design Firm

Majima Design

Client

Gulliver

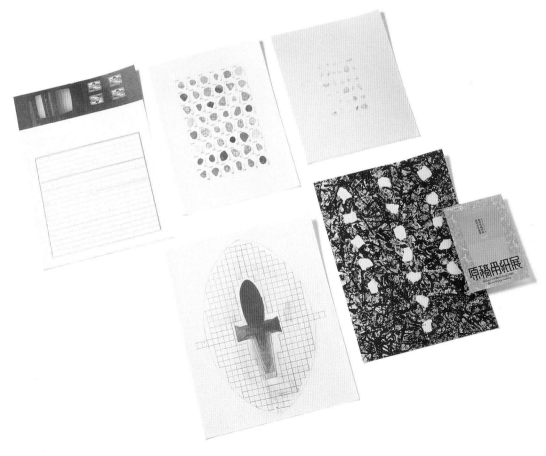

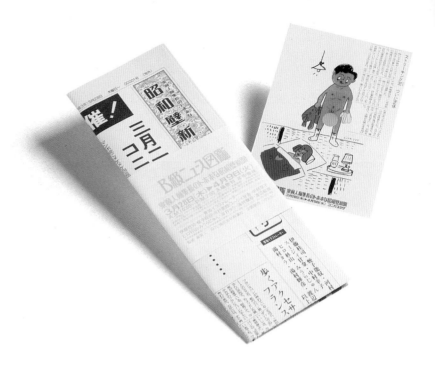

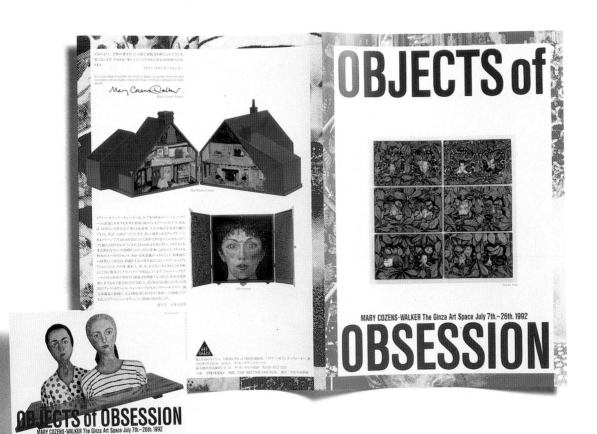

MARY COZENS-WALKER
"OBJECTS OF OBSESSION"
メアリー・カズンズ＝ウォーカー展
"愛と生活のオブジェ"

JAPAN 1992

Art Director

Shuji Kawasaki

Designer

Tetsuo Ozaki

Illustrator

Mary Cozens-Walker

Design Firm

Heads

Client

**Shiseido Division of
Corporate Culture**

P.112
EXHIBITION &
ILLUSTRATED WALL NEWSPAPER
"THE B-CLASS"
展示会と壁新聞
"Ｂ級ニュース図鑑"

JAPAN 1991

Creative Director

H'action

Art Director

Katsunori Aoki

Designer

Katsunori Aoki

Illustrators

Keiji Ito

Norikazu Ebisu

Yousuke Kawamura

Suzie Amagane

Sachiko Nakamura

Hiro Sugiyama

Jun Miura

Tara Yumura

Teruhiko Yumura

Kazuhiro Watanabe

Copywriter

Asato Izumi

Design Firm

H'action

Client

Konica Plaza

THE HAWAIIAN SHIRT EXHIBITION
アロハシャツ展

ハワイが最もハワイだった日々の記憶。

JAPAN 1991

Art Director

Masaaki Hiromura

Designers

Masaaki Hiromura

Takafumi Kusagaya

Photographer

Masayuki Hayashi

Planner

Seigo Kaneko

Design Firm

Hiromura Design Office

Client

Ryubo

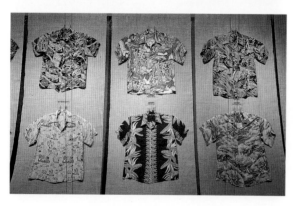

MASAAKI HIROMURA EXHIBITION
"WIRED"
広村正彰展 "WIRED"

JAPAN 1991
Art Director
Masaaki Hiromura
Designer
Masaaki Hiromura
Photographer
Masaaki Hayashi
Design Firm
Hiromura Design Office
Client
Tokyo Designers Space

JAGDA NEW ARTIST AWARD
EXHIBITION '91 & '92
JAGDA 新人賞受賞作家作品展

JAPAN 1992

Art Directors

Masato Oki

Kotaro Hirano

Ken Miki

Designers

Masato Oki

Kotaro Hirano

Ken Miki

Client

Creation Gallery G8

JUNKO MADA EXHIBITION
"ECOLOGICAL PIECES"

馬田純子作品展
"ECOLOGICAL PIECES"

JAPAN 1991

Art Director

Kentaro Honzawa

Designer

Kazuhiko Tabata

Photographer

Yoshikazu Okamura

Artist

Junko Mada

Client

Creation Gallery G8

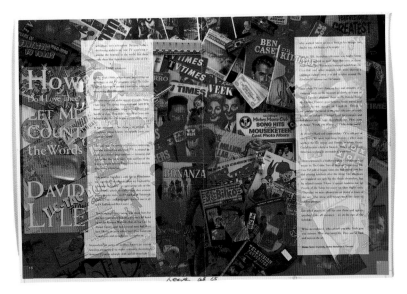

EXHIBITION
"T.V. TIMES-35 YEARS OF
WATCHING TELEVISION"
展示会
"T.V. TIMES-35 YEARS OF
WATCHING TELEVISION"

AUSTRALIA 1992

Creative Director

Kevin Wilkins

Art Directors

David Watson

Kevin Wilkins

Designer

Kevin Wilkins

Photographer

Richie Nicholson

Illustrators

Sarah Viarcoe

Tim Whitely

Copywriters

David Watson

Dennise Ccrrkan

Design Firm

Siren

Client

**Museum of Contemporary
Art Sydney**

**CHRIS NASH
DANCE PHOTO EXHIBITION**
クリス・ナッシュ写真展

JAPAN 1990

Art Director

Tomohiko Nagakura

Designer

Tomohiko Nagakura

Photographer

Chris Nash

Design Firm

Sun-AD

Client

Parco

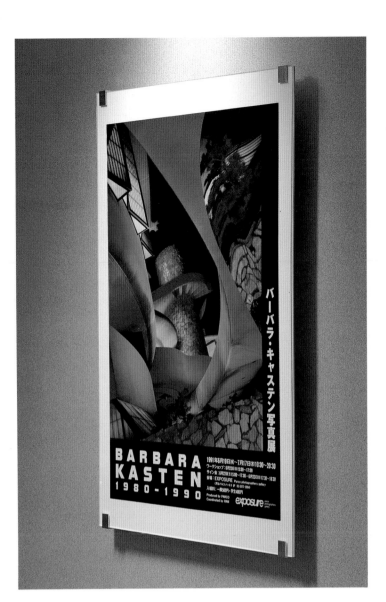

BARBARA KASTEN 1980-1990
バーバラ・キャステン写真展

JAPAN 1991

Art Director

Hideyuki Taguchi

Photographer

Barbara Kasten

Design Firm

RAM

Client

Parco

PHOTO EXHIBITION
"SHINJUKU SHINOYAMA KISHIN"
写真展 "篠山紀信 SHINJUKU"

JAPAN 1991

Art Director

Katsuhiro Kinoshita

Designer

Katsuhiro Kinoshita

Photographer

Kishin Shinoyama

Copywriter

Akio Nakamori

Design Firm

Design Club

Client

Galerie Tokoro

NORIAKI YOKOSUKA
PHOTO EXHIBITION
"DAS TRIADICSCHE BALLETT"
横須賀功光写真展
"時間の庭 - 結晶化した
トリアディック・バレエ"

JAPAN 1990

Art Director

Katsuhiko Shibuya

Designer

Katsuhiko Shibuya

Photographer

Noriaki Yokosuka

Design Firm

Shiseido

Client

Parco

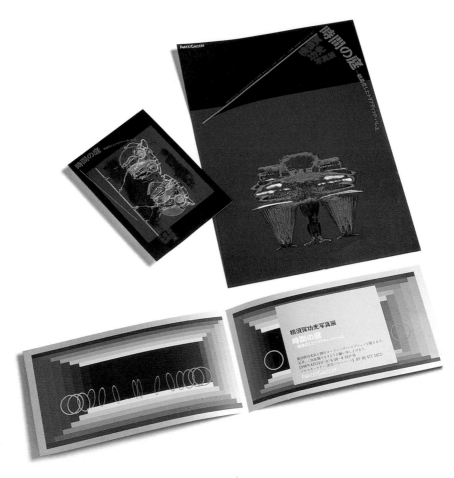

SHINRO OHTAKE NEW WORKS
大竹伸朗 新作展

JAPAN 1988
Art Director
Katsuhiro Kinoshita
Designer
Katsuhiro Kinoshita
Artist
Shinro Ohtake
Design Firm
Design Club
Client
The Seibu Department Store

**GARY HILL EXHIBITION CATALOGUE
"I BELIEVE IT IS AN IMAGE"**
ゲイリー・ヒル
ビデオ・インスタレーション展

JAPAN 1992

Creative Directors

Etsuko Watari

Koichi Watari

Designer

Ichiro Tanida

Photographers

Mark B Mcloughlin

Georges Poncet

Ryoji Watabe

Client

**Watari-UM
The Watari Museum of
Contemporary Art**

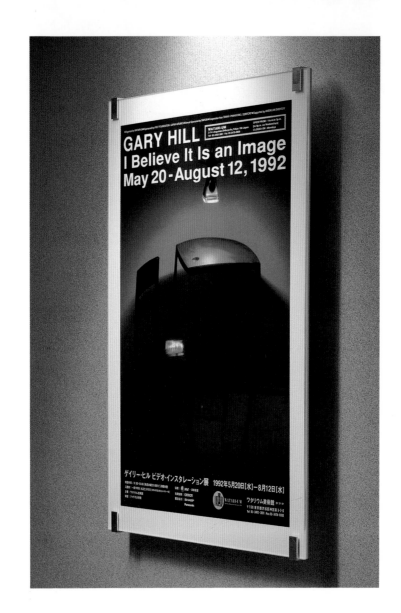

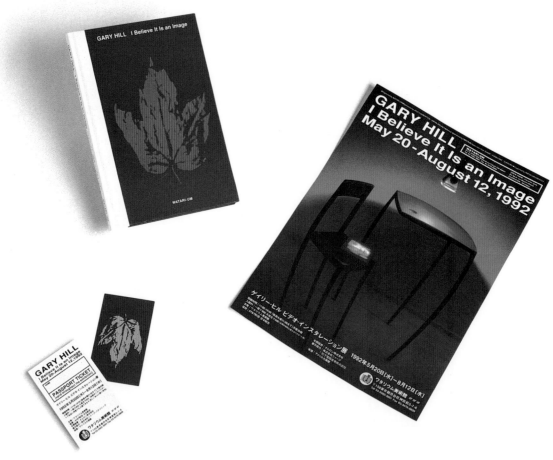

JAPAN PRINT '91
ジャパン プリント '91

JAPAN 1991

Art Director

Koichi Sato

Designer

Koichi Sato

Client

Dai-Nippon Printing

ART EXHIBITION
"3 RAUMINSTALLATIONEN"
美術展
"3 RAUMINSTALLATIONEN"

SWITZERLAND 1990

Art Director

Michael Baviera

Design Firm

BBV

Client

Kunsthaus Zürich

ART EXHIBITION
"KONKRETE KUNST"
美術展
"KONKRETE KUNST"

SWITZERLAND 1991

Art Director

Michael Baviera

Design Firm

BBV

Client

Kunsthaus Glarus

JOSEF ALBERS
GRUPPE X
ROMAN CLEMENS
ALFRED AUER
FRITZ GLARNER
ARTURO DI MARIA
CAMILLE GRAESER
MICHAEL BAVIERA
GOTTFRIED HONEGGER
WILLI GOETZ
VERENA LOEWENSBERG
HEY HEUSSLER
BARNETT NEWMAN
RUDOLF HURNI
BRIDGET RILEY
MÜLLER-EMIL
RÜCKRIEM
RAFAEL PEREZ
SOL LEWITT
RUTH SENN-WETLI

WORLD GRAPHICA 1990
ワールド グラフィカ 1990

JAPAN 1990

Art Director

Katsuhiro Kinoshita

Designer

Katsuhiro Kinoshita

Artists

Makoto Saito

Grapus

Design Firm

Design Club

Client

Alpha Cubic Gallery

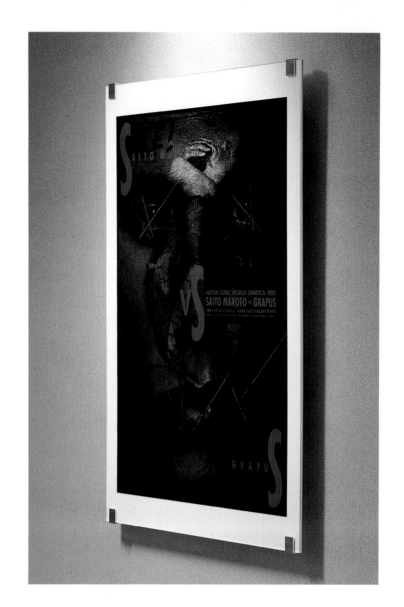

APRIL GREIMAN EXHIBITION
エイプリル・グレイマン展

JAPAN 1991

Creative Director
Seiji Koseki

Art Director
Tatsuomi Majima

Designer
Tatsuomi Majima

Space Layout
Ikushi Tomita

Design Firm
Majima Design

Client
Gulliver

PEP EXHIBITION
PEP 展

JAPAN 1991

Creative Director

Seiji Koseki

Art Director

Tatsuomi Majima

Designers

Tatsuomi Majima

Kyoko Akatsuka

Hiroko Murata

Copywriter

Megumi Yunoki

Artist

Robert Longo

Design Firm

Majima Design

Client

Gulliver

MUSEUM & GALLERY EXHIBITIONS

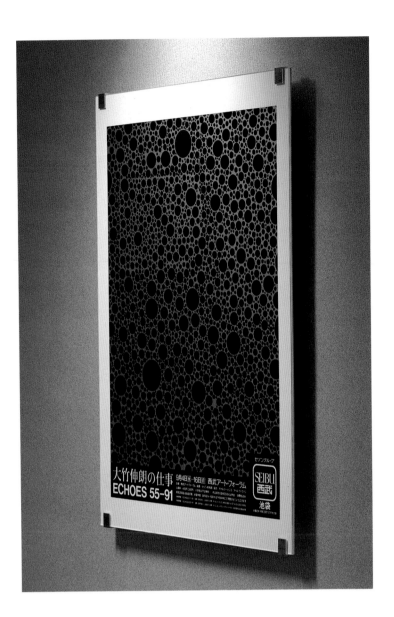

"ECHOES"
WORKS OF SHINRO OHTAKE
"エコーズ"
大竹伸朗の仕事

JAPAN 1991

Creative Directors

Shinro Ohtake

Katsuhiro Kinoshita

Kyoichi Tsuzuki

Art Director

Katsuhiro Kinoshita

Copywriter

Kyoichi Tsuzuki

Artist

Shinro Ohtake

Design Firm

Design Club

Client

The Seibu Department Store

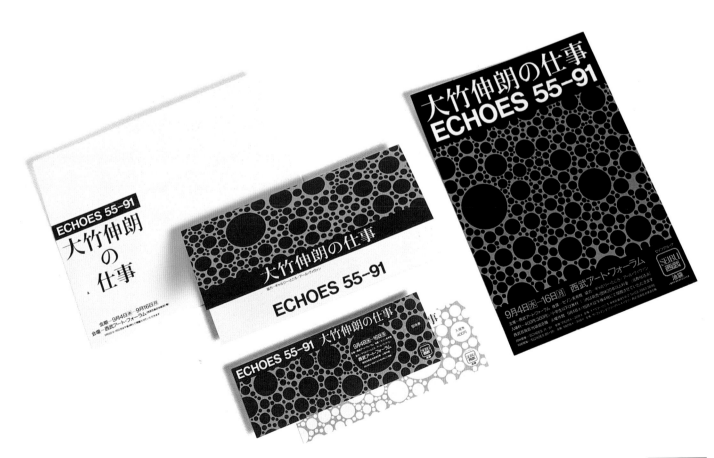

**CRANBROOK DESIGN
THE NEW DISCOURSE**
クランブルック デザイン日本展

JAPAN 1991

Art Director

Katherine McCoy

Designers

Scott Makela

Ryoji Ohashi

Design Firm

Sugarpot GR

Client

**Executive Committee of
Cranbrook Design in Japan**

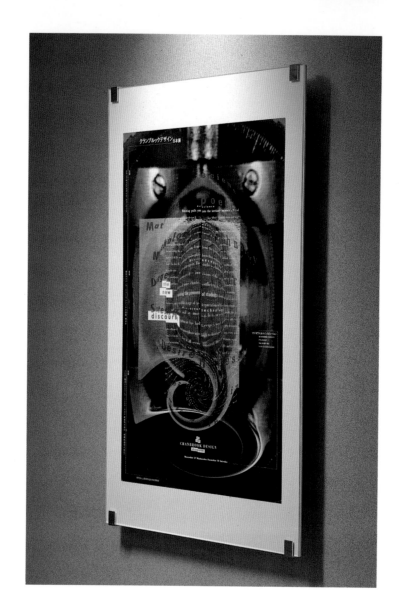

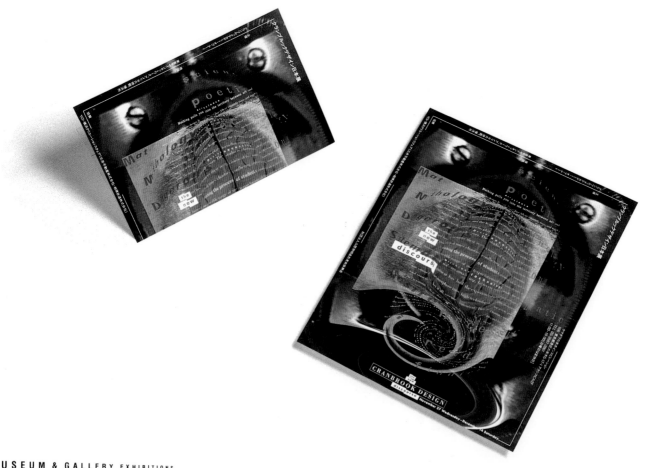

STEVE REICH AND MUSICIANS
スティーヴ・ライヒと音楽家たち

JAPAN 1991
Art Director
Kenzo Izutani
Designers
Kenzo Izutani
Aki Hirai
Design Firm
Kenzo Izutani Office
Clients
Asahi Newspaper
Bunkamura

MALCOLM GARRETT
"ULTERIOR MOTIFS"
マルコム・ギャレット
"ウルテリア・モチーフ"展

JAPAN 1991

Art Director

Malcolm Garrett

Designer

Malcolm Garrett

Design Firm

Assorted Images

Client

Parco

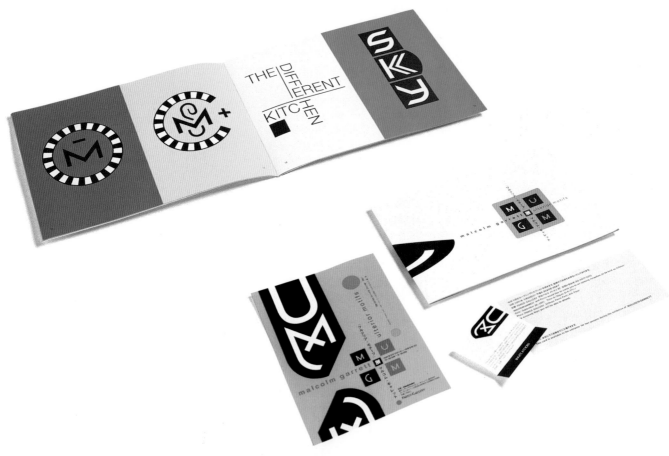

PETER SAVILLE GRAPHICS FROM PSA TO PENTAGRAM
ピーター・サヴィル展

JAPAN 1991

Art Director

Peter Saville

Designer

Bret Wickens

Design Firm

Pentagram

Client

Parco

JOSEPH BEUYS
EXHIBITION CATALOGUE
"BEYOND THE BORDER TO EURASIA"
ヨーゼフ・ボイス展

JAPAN 1991

Creative Directors

Etsuko Watari

Koichi Watari

Designer

Kenji Osanai

Design Firm

Autobahn

Client

**Watari-UM
The Watari Museum of
Contemporary Art**

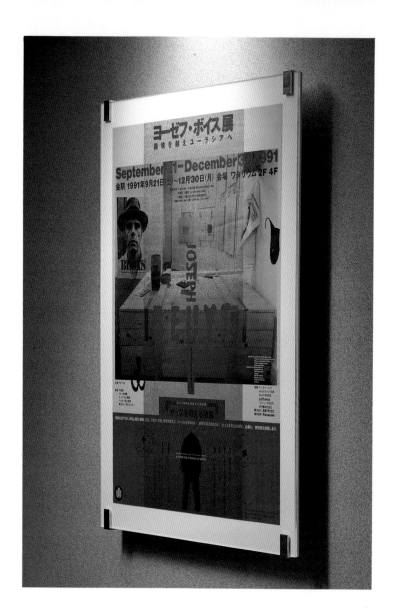

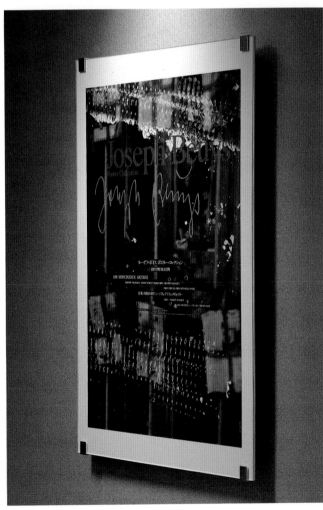

**JOSEPH BEUYS:
POSTER COLLECTION**

ヨーゼフ・ボイス：
ポスターコレクション

JAPAN 1991

Art Director

Kijuro Yahagi

Designer

Kijuro Yahagi

Photographer

Kijuro Yahagi

Client

Kawasaki City Museum

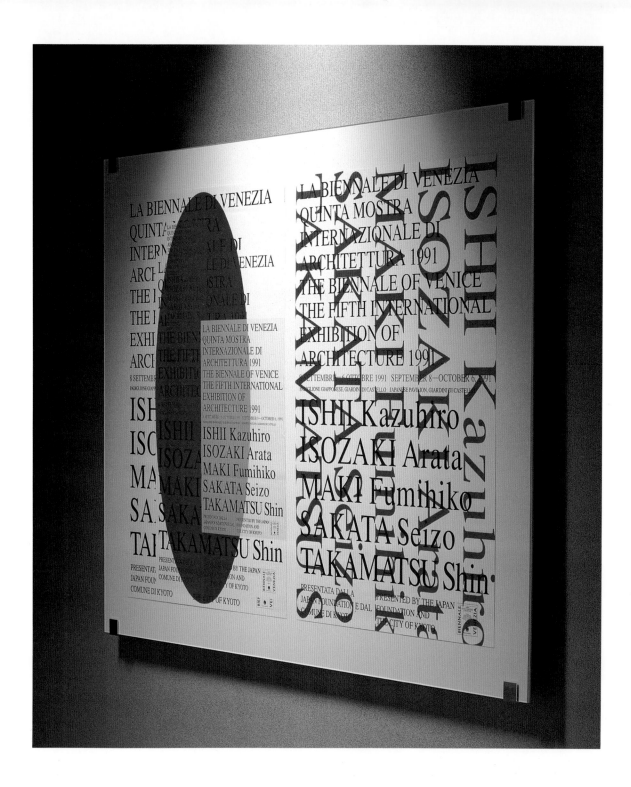

"THE BIENNALE OF VENICE"
THE FIFTH INTERNATIONAL
EXHIBITION OF ARCHITECTURE 1991
1991 ヴェニス・ビエンナーレ
第5回国際建築展

JAPAN 1991

Art Director

Kijuro Yahagi

Designer

Kijuro Yahagi

Client

The Japan Foundation

EXHIBITION
"MARCEL DUNCHAMP GRAPICS"
"マルセル・デュシャン・
グラフィックス " 展

JAPAN 1991

Art Director

Kijuro Yahagi

Designer

Kijuro Yahagi

Client

BIGI Art Space

EXHIBITION
"REMOVABLE REALITY"
"脱着するリアリティ"展

JAPAN 1992

Art Director

Ichiro Higashiizumi

Designers

Nobuharu Noto

Shuichi Miyagishi

Megumi Takeuchi

Artists

Masaki Fujihata

Keiichi Irie

Editors

Gabin Itoh

Urban Design Research

Design Firm

Huia Media Design

Client

NTT

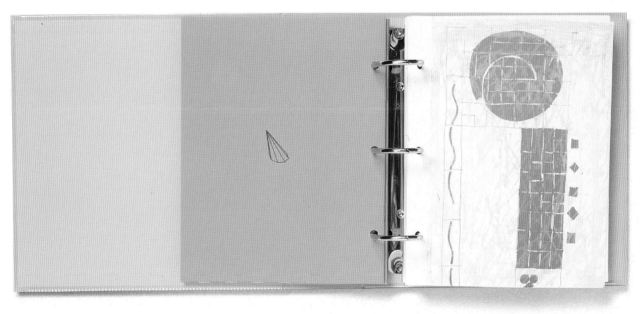

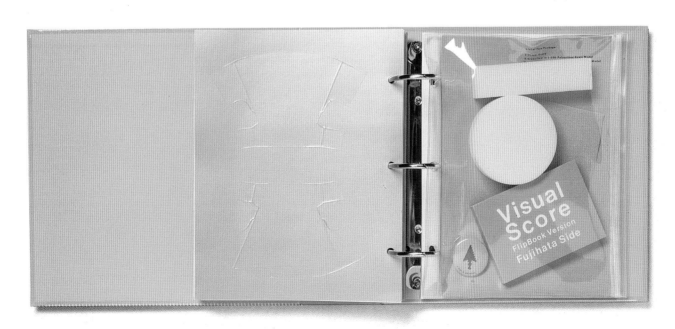

ART EXHIBITION
"RAUMA BIENNALE BALTICUM 1992"
美術展
"RAUMA BIENNALE BALTICUM 1992"

FINLAND 1992

Art Director

Jari Silvennoinen

Photographer

Jari Silvennoinen

Client

The Rauma Art Museum

SOUND INSTALLATION
"WIND" "FOUR DEVICES"
音の空間シリーズ
"ウインド" "四つの装置"

JAPAN 1991

Art Director

Hironori Murai

Designers

Hironori Murai

Rumiko Kanesaka

Artists

Rolf Julius

Takehisa Kosugi

Client

P3 Art and Environment

BERNARD FAUCON EXHIBITION
"ÉLOGE DOMANNEQUIN"
ベルナール・フォコン展
"偶像礼讃"

JAPAN 1991

Art Director

Yasuo Kuboki

Designer

Yuji Kimura

Photographer

Bernard Faucon

Client

Parco

P.142
BERNARD FAUCON EXHIBITION
"LES IDOLES ET LES SACRIFICES"
ベルナール・フォコン展
"偶像と生贄"

JAPAN 1991

Art Director

Yasuo Kuboki

Designer

Yuji Kimura

Photographer

Bernard Faucon

Client

Parco

CZECHO AND SLOVAK
CONTEMPORARY PHOTOGRAPHIC
EXHIBITION "FANCY ROAD"
チェコスロバキア現代写真展
"虚日の揺らめき"

JAPAN 1991

Art Director

Kenzo Izutani

Designer

Kenzo Izutani

Photographer

Miro Svolík

Design Firm

Kenzo Izutani Office

Client

Parco

**FRANK LOYD WRIGHT
RETROSPECTIVE**
フランク・ロイド・ライト回顧展

JAPAN 1991

Art Director

Yoshinobu Nochioka

Designer

Yoshinobu Nochioka

Design Firm

Southpire

Client

Yokohama Museum of Art

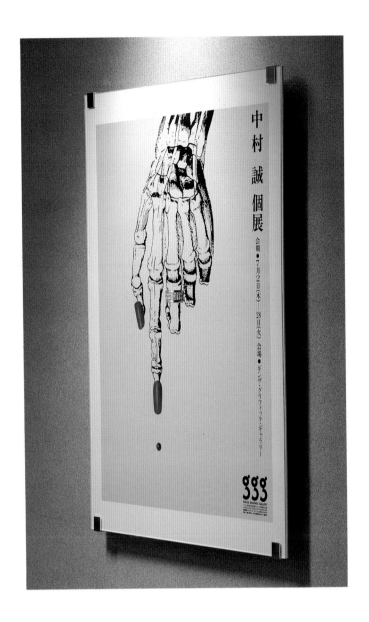

**MAKOTO NAKAMURA
POSTER EXHIBITION**
中村 誠 個展

JAPAN 1990-1992
Art Director
Makoto Nakamura
Designer
Makoto Nakamura
Design Firm
Shiseido
Client
Ginza Graphic Gallery

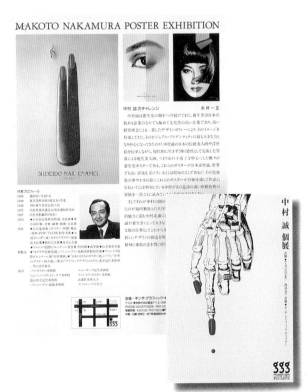

THE 4TH TOKYO TDC EXHIBITION
第4回
東京タイポディレクターズクラブ展

JAPAN 1991

Art Director

Kaoru Kasai

Designer

Kaoru Kasai

Design Firm

Sun-AD

Client

Ginza Graphic Gallery

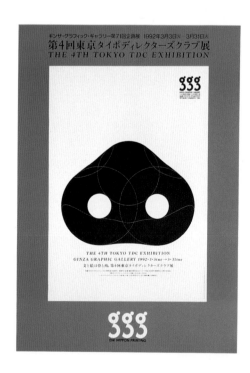

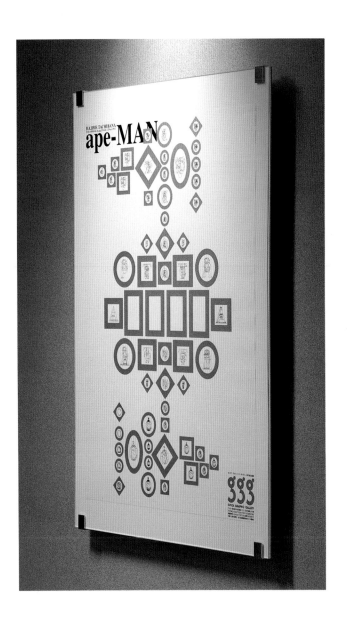

**HAJIME TACHIBANA
FIRST EXHIBITION**
立花ハジメ 初の個展

JAPAN 1991-1992
Art Director
Hajime Tachibana
Designer
Hajime Tachibana
Design Firm
Hajime Tachibana Design
Client
Ginza Graphic Gallery

EXHIBITION
"COLLABORATION SERIES"
展覧会
"コラボレーションシリーズ
1×1は無限大"

JAPAN 1992

Art Director

Osamu Sato

Designer

Osamu Sato

Illustrator

Osamu Sato

Producer

Yoko Niki

Client

Illuminat (Tierrart)

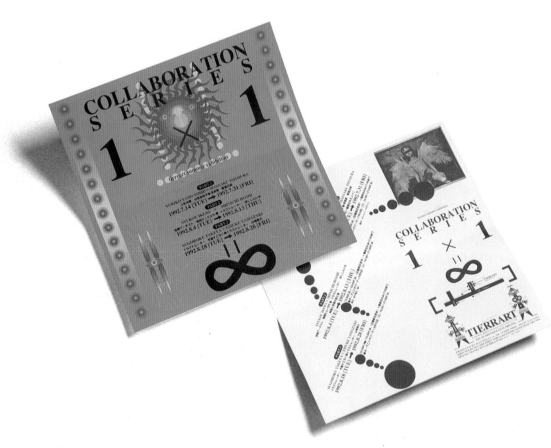

EXHIBITION
"THE AMBIENT COLLECTION"
展覧会
"アンビエントコレクション"

JAPAN 1991

Art Director

Osamu Sato

Designer

Osamu Sato

Illustrator

Osamu Sato

Producer

Yoko Niki

Client

Illuminat (Tierrart)

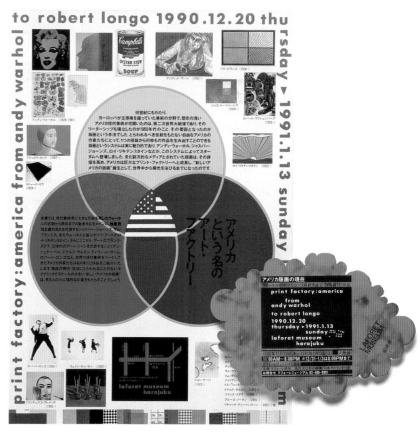

PRINT FACTORY:AMERICA
アメリカ版画の現在

JAPAN 1990

Art Director

Yasunori Yotsugi

Designers

Yasunori Yotsugi

Masakazu Kitayama

Photographer

Yasunori Yotsugi

Client

Laforet Harajuku

GIRAFFE CLOUD EXHIBITION
"KNOCKIN' ON HEAVEN'S DOOR"
ジオクラウド展
"ノッキン オン ヘヴンズ ドア"

JAPAN 1992

Creative Director

Giraffe Cloud

Photographer

Giraffe Cloud

Artist

Giraffe Cloud

Client

Hypercritical

ART EXHIBITION "ZONES OF LOVE"
美術展 "ZONES OF LOVE"

AUSTRALIA 1991

Art Director

Kevin Wilkins

Designer

Tim Whitely

Photographer

Richie Nicholson

Illustrator

Tim Whitely

Copywriter

Judy Anear

Design Firm

Siren

Client

**Museum of
Contemporary Art Sydney**

TADAYUKI NAITO
PHOTO EXHIBITION
"SAKURA-COSM"
内藤忠行写真展
"SAKURA-COSM"

JAPAN 1990

Art Director

Toshio Shiratani

Designer

Toshio Shiratani

Photographer

Tadayuki Naito

Brush Writing

Aiko Kudo

Client

Laforet Harajuku

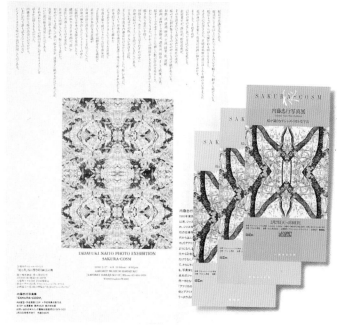

EXHIBITION
"NEO INDÉPENDANTS 1992"
展覧会
"ネオ・アンデパンダン 1992"

JAPAN 1992

Art Director

Hirosuke Ueno

Designer

Hirosuke Ueno

Illustrator

Hirosuke Ueno

Client

Hypercritical

THEATER PLAY
"ONE WEEK"
劇団公演
"ナビと奇跡の一週間"

JAPAN 1987

Art Director

Koichi Sato

Designer

Koichi Sato

Client

**Theatrical Company
Seinenza**

"MINE & GAG
CLOWN PERFORMANCE"
ミミクリーチ
"クラウン・パフォーマンス"

JAPAN 1990

Art Director

Yasunori Yotsugi

Designers

Yasunori Yotsugi

Masakazu Kitayama

Client

Laforet Harajuku

1. THEATRE PLAY
"TAMASABURO BANDO"
坂東玉三郎公演

JAPAN 1992

Art Director

Ikko Tanaka

Designer

Taro Matsuyoshi

Photographer

Kishin Shinoyama

Client

Ginza Saison Theatre

2. THEATRE PLAY
"TITUS ANDRONICUS"
劇場公演
"タイタス・アンドロニカス"

JAPAN 1992

Art Director

Ikko Tanaka

Designer

Taro Matsuyoshi

Illustrator

Akira Uno

Client

Ginza Saison Theatre

3. THEATRE PLAY
"ONNA KOROSHI ABURANO JIGOKU"
劇場公演 "女殺油地獄"

JAPAN 1990

Art Director

Ikko Tanaka

Designer

Taro Matsuyoshi

Illustrator

Haruo Takino

Copywriter

Kazui Kawakami

Client

Ginza Saison Theatre

4. THEATRE PLAY
"LA TRAGÉDIE DE CARMEN"
劇場公演 "カルメンの悲劇"

JAPAN 1987

Art Director

Ikko Tanaka

Designer

Kan Akita

Illustrator

Haruo Takino

Copywriter

Kazui Kawakami

Client

Ginza Saison Theatre

1

2

3

4

ENTERTAINMENT

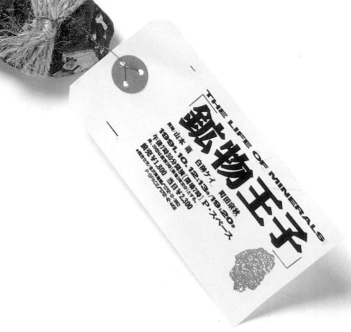

TEATER PLAY
"THE LIFE OF MINERALS"
劇団公演 "鉱物王子"

JAPAN 1991

Art Director

Atsushi Minami

Designer

Hideaki Toda

Artist

Atsushi Minami

Design Firm

Blue

Client

Kanazawa Butoh Kan

1. THEATRE PLAY
"NIGHTS OF AN ANATOMY"

劇団公演 "人体模型の夜"

2. THEATER PLAY "THE BABY"

劇団公演 "ベイビーさん"

3. THEATRE PLAY
"1RO CHAN GOES AGAIN"

劇団公演
"一郎ちゃんがもっといく"

4. THEATRE PLAY
"HOW MANY ANGELS
ON A SPOON?"

劇団公演
"スプーンの上に
天使何人とまれるか"

5. THEATRE PLAY
"KO-CHU-TEN-KI-BUN"

劇団公演 "壷中天奇聞"

6. THEATRE PLAY
"KA-CHO-TEN-SHO"

劇団公演 "花彫天書"

JAPAN 1992

Art Director

Shinnosuke Sugisaki

Designer

Mitsuharu Kimura

Illustrator

Michio Hisauchi

Design Firm

Shinnosuke

Client

Nakajima Ramo Office

HARAJUKU BUNRAKU
"SONEZAKI SHINJU"

第1回原宿文楽
"曾根崎心中"

JAPAN 1987

Creative Director

Syozo Tsurumoto

Art Director

Ichiro Higashiizumi

Copywriter

Takashi Takemura

Design Firm

Huia Media Design

Client

Laforet Harajuku

THE 6th HARAJUKU BUNRAKU
"TOMOMORI"

第6回原宿文楽
"碇知盛"

JAPAN 1992

Art Directors

Takayuki Terakado

Takashi Ota

Designer

Takashi Ota

Illustrator

Takayuki Terakado

Client

Laforet Harajuku

TOKYO GINGADŌ
"BRAIN STORM"

東京ギンガ堂
"ブレイン・ストーム"

JAPAN 1992

Creative Director

Nousei Shinagawa

Art Director

Katsunori Aoki

Designer

Katsunori Aoki

Photographer

Koichi Ikegame

Illustrator

Katsunori Aoki

Copywriter

Nousei Shinagawa

Client

Theatrical Project
Tokyo Ginga Dō

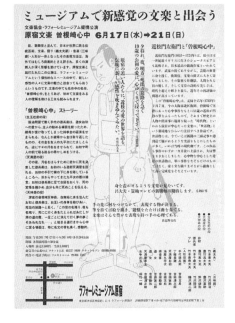

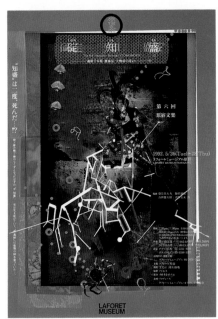

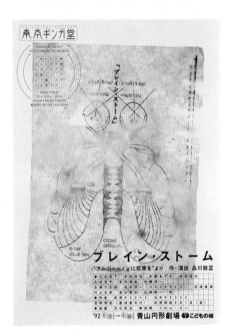

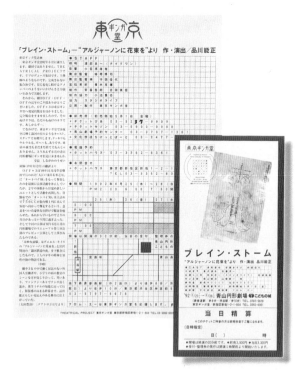

THEATER PLAY "APPARE"
劇団公演 "天晴れ"

JAPAN 1988

Art Director

Keisuke Nagatomo

Designer

Masayuki Takahashi

Photographer

Masaaki Miyazawa

Design Firm

K-Two

Client

Aoitori

THEATER PLAY "FUREN DANCE"
劇団公演 "風煉ダンス"

JAPAN 1992

Art Director

Seiji Furukawa

Designer

Seiji Furukawa

Illustrator

Seiji Furukawa

Client

Furen Dance

"KODO GATHERING"
JAPANESE DRUM
"鼓童"

JAPAN 1991

Art Director

Keisuke Nagatomo

Designer

Masayuki Takahashi

Illustrator

Seitaro Kuroda

Design Firm

K-Two

Client

Kodo

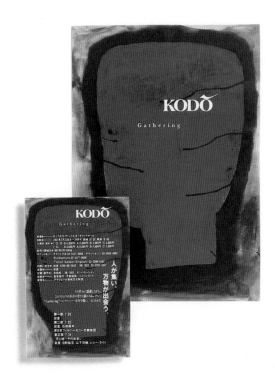

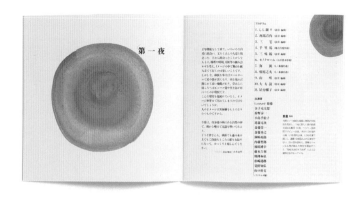

THEATER PLAY "MONTAGE"
劇団公演 "モンタージュ"

JAPAN 1991

Art Director

Keisuke Nagatomo

Designer

Masayuki Takahashi

Photographer

Naoo Kumagai

Object Designer

Yasuko Ohtomo

Design Firm

K-Two

Client

Yū◉Kikai / Zenjidō Theater

FILM "BYOUIN E IKO"
映画"病院へ行こう"

JAPAN 1989

Art Director

Keisuke Nagatomo

Designer

Takashi Nomura

Illustrator

Yukio Asaga

Design Firm

K-Two

Client

Tohei

YUKIHIRO TAKAHASHI CONCERT
"A NIGHT IN THE NEXT LIFE"
高橋幸宏コンサート
"アナイト イン ザ ネクスト ライフ"

JAPAN 1991

Art Director

Mitsuo Shindo

Designers

Koichi Fujikawa

Satoshi Nakamura

Photographers

Kenji Miura

Kiyonori Okuyama

Hair Make

Mikiko Honda

Design Firm

Contemporary Production

Client

Office Intenźio

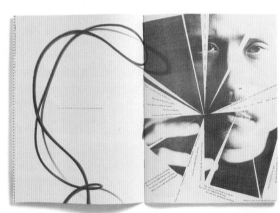

YOSHITAKA MINAMI LIVE TWO
MONTHS AHEAD
南　佳孝コンサート

JAPAN 1991
Art Director
Yoichi Fujii
Designer
Maki Shinoda
Photographer
Noriyuki Usui
Client
C.S.Artist

**NOKKO TOKYO LIVE
"CLUB HALLELUJAH"**

ノッコ・トーキョー ライブ
"クラブ・ハレルヤ"

JAPAN 1992

Creative Directors

Nokko

Mariko Nakayama

Art Director

Shinsuke Mochida

Designer

Shinsuke Mochida

Photographer

Hideo Kanno

Design Firm

Sindbad Design

Client

Shinko Music Publishing

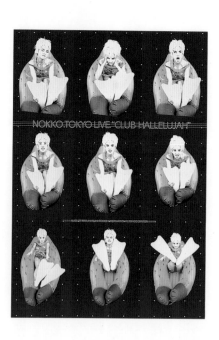

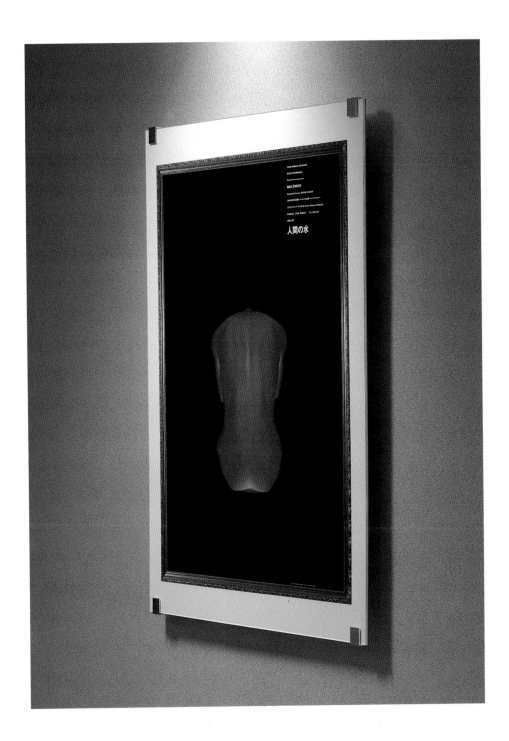

DANCE PERFORMANCE
"MAN WATER"
舞踏パフォーマンス
"人間の水"

JAPAN 1990

Art Director

Yoshiro Kajitani

Designer

Yoshiro Kajitani

Photographer

Hitoshi Iwakiri

Design Firm

Kajitani Design Room

Client

Kohzensha

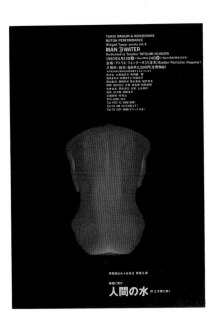

**DANCE PERFORMANCE
"BLUE PILLAR"**
舞踏パフォーマンス
"青い柱"

JAPAN 1991

Art Director

Yoshiro Kajitani

Designer

Yoshiro Kajitani

Photographer

Hitoshi Iwakiri

Design Firm

Kajitani Design Room

Client

Kohzensha

PERFORMANCE SUARAGUNG
"JEGOG"

スアール・アグン
"ジェゴグ" 公演

JAPAN 1992

Creative Director

Hitoshi Nambu

Art Director

Michiko Arakawa

Designer

Michiko Arakawa

Photographer

Shoichi Sakomizu

Design Firm

Kajitani Design Room

Client

Tokyo P/N

**DANCE CONCERTS
"DANCES FOR WAVE HILL"**
ダンスコンサート
"DANCES FOR WAVE HILL"

USA 1991

Creative Director

Gail Rigelhaupt

Designer

Gail Rigelhaupt

Photographer

Philip Trager

Copywriter

Elise Bernhardt

Design Firm

Rigelhaupt Design

Client

Dancing In The Streets and Wavehill

**INVITATION OF BALLET CONCERTS
"NUTCRACKER BALL"**
バレエ公演
"NUTCRACKER BALL" への招待

USA 1991

Art Director

Jack Anderson

Designers

Jack Anderson

Jani Drewfs

Illustrator

Nancy Gellos

Copywriter

Pamela Mason-Davey

Design Firm

Hornall Anderson Design Works

Client

Pacific Northwest Ballet

PERFORMANCE BY
A CLASSICAL AND
CONTEMPORARY MUSIC GROUP
"ENDYMION ENSEMBLE"
クラシックおよび
現代音楽グループ演奏
"ENDYMION ENSEMBLE"

UK 1991

Art Director

John Rushworth

Designers

John Rushworth

Vince Frost

Design Firm

Pentagram Design

Client

Endymion Ensemble

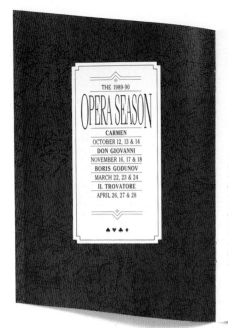

PROMOTION OF AN OPERA
オペラのプロモーション

USA 1988

Art Director

Eric Rickabaugh

Designer

Eric Rickabaugh

Illustrators

Michael David Brown

Mark Riedy

Copywriter

Rosa Stolz

Design Firm

Rickabaugh Graphics

Client

Opera / Columbus

AUSTIN LYRIC OPERA
オースチン・リリック オペラ公演

USA 1991

Art Director

**Richard Whittington /
Whittington Design**

Designer

**Richard Whittington /
Whittington Design**

Illustrator

Melissa Grimes

Copywriter

Foster Hurley

Design Firm

Whittington Design

Client

Austin Lyric Opera

CONCERT "JIM BEARD"
コンサート "JIM BEARD"

THE NETHERLANDS 1991

Designer

Boy Bastiaens

Photographer

Marc Lochs

Illustrator

Boy Bastiaens

Client

Take Five Concerts

ENTERTAINMENT

FESTIVAL
"BUSKERS FESTIVAL"
大道芸人フェスティバル
"BUSKERS FESTIVAL"

ITALY 1988

Art Director

Graziano Uillani

Designer

Ilde Ianigro

Photographer

Graziano Uillani

Client

**Assogazione Buskers
Festival**

FASHION SHOW
"LCF PUBLICITY 1992"
ファッションショー
"LCF PUBLICITY 1992"

UK 1992

Art Directors

Paul West

Paula Benson

Designers

Paul West

Paula Benson

Design Firm

Form

Client

London College Fashion /
The London Institute

AWARDS EVENT
"A TOKEN OF OUR APPRECIATION"
表彰イベント
"A TOKEN OF OUR APPRECIATION"

USA 1990

Art Director

John Sayles

Designer

John Sayles

Copywriter

Wendy Lyons

Design Firm

Sayles Graphic Design

Client

Sayles Graphic Design

FREE OUTDOOR CONCERTS SERIES
"MUSIC IN THE AIR"
無料屋外コンサートシリーズ
"MUSIC IN THE AIR"

USA 1987-1992

Art Director

Eric Rickabaugh

Designer

Erick Rickabaugh

Photographer

Roman Sapecki

Illustrators

**Eric Rickabaugh /
Michael Tennyson Smith**

Design Firm

Rickabaugh Graphics

Client

The City of Columbus

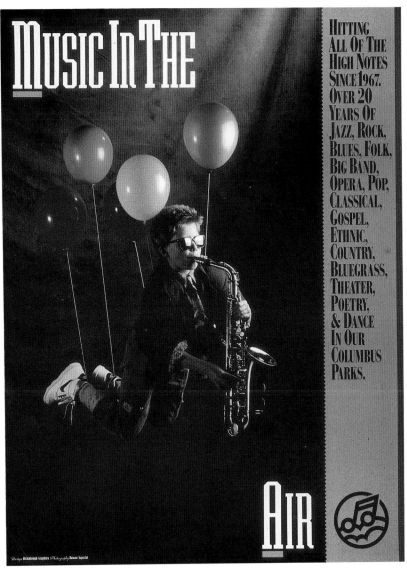

MUSIC IN THE

AIR

HITTING ALL OF THE HIGH NOTES SINCE 1967. OVER 20 YEARS OF JAZZ, ROCK, BLUES, FOLK, BIG BAND, OPERA, POP, CLASSICAL, GOSPEL, ETHNIC, COUNTRY, BLUEGRASS, THEATER, POETRY, & DANCE IN OUR COLUMBUS PARKS.

**CASABLANCA
50th ANNIVERSARY**

放送システム会社の
映画"カサブランカ"
50周年記念イベント

USA 1992

Creative Director

Joe Swaney

Designer

Tracy Sabin

Illustrator

Tracy Sabin

Design Firm

Sabin Design

Client

Turner Broadcasting System

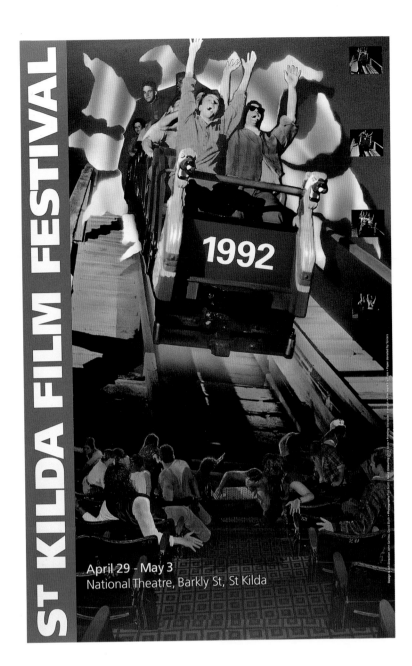

"ST. KILDA FILM FESTIVAL 1992"
映画祭
"ST. KILDA FILM FESTIVAL 1992"

AUSTRALIA 1992

Art Directors

John Sellitto

David Blyth

Designers

John Sellitto

David Blyth

Photographer

Tim Scott

Hand Colouring

Chris Sikos

Design Firm

Sellitto Blyth Design

Client

City of St. Kilda

CENTENARY FESTIVAL OF
THE JAPAN SOCIETY
"JAPAN FESTIVAL-
THE GRAND SUMO TOURNAMENT"
日本協会百年祭記念イベント
"JAPAN FESTIVAL-
大相撲トーナメント"

UK 1991

Art Director

John McConnell

Designers

John McConnell

Jason Godfrey

Design Firm

Pentagram Design

Client

Japan Society

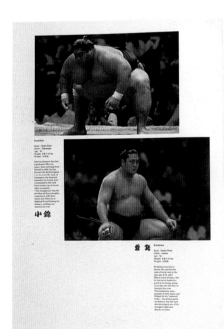

HIROSHIMA 1987-1997
ヒロシマ 1987-1997

JAPAN 1987

Creative Director

Shigeo Goto

Art Director

Tsuguya Inoue

Designers

Tsuguya Inoue

Beans

Photographer

Sachiko Kuru

Design Firm

Beans

Client

**Hiroshima
1987-1997 Project**

HIROSHIMA 1987-1997
NOTICE:COMPLETION OF
AN EXTENDED CARE FACILITY
ヒロシマ 1987-1997
養護施設完成のおしらせ

JAPAN 1992

Creative Director

Shigeo Goto

Art Director

Ryoichi Seino

Designer

Ryoichi Seino

Photographer

Ryoichi Seino

Design Firm

Ink Spots

Client

**Hiroshima
1987-1997 Project**

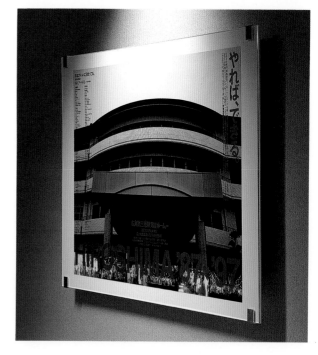

HIROSHIMA '91
ヒロシマ '91

JAPAN 1991
Creative Director
Shigeo Goto
Art Director
Ryoichi Seino
Designer
Ryoichi Seino
Illustrator
Seitaro Kuroda
Copywriter
Shigeo Goto
Design Firm
Ink Spots
Client
**Hiroshima
1987-1997 Project**

SOUTHEAST ASIAN FESTIVAL'92
東南アジア祭 '92

JAPAN 1992

Designers

Kohei Sugiura

Akihiko Tanimura

Photograph Quotation

You Takeuchi Collection

Printing

Toppan Printing

Client

**Southeast Asian Festival'92
Executive Committee**

FLORAL COSMOLOGY
花宇宙

JAPAN 1992
Designer
Akihiko Tanimura
Photographer
Takanori Sugino
Illustrators
Teiji Asanuma
Takumi Yamamoto
Space Layout
Shoichi Akazaki
Akinori Horiya
Atsusi Sato
Takumi Yamamoto
Printing
Toppan Printing
Client
**Southeast Asian Festival'92
Executive Committee**

MUSIC FESTIVAL "MOTHER"
"一万人の5本締め"

JAPAN 1992

Creative Director

Shigeo Goto

Art Director

Takashi Miyagawa

Designer

The Expression's

Photographer

Kenji Miura

Copywriter

Shigeo Goto

Design Firm

The Expression's

Client

Mother Enterprise

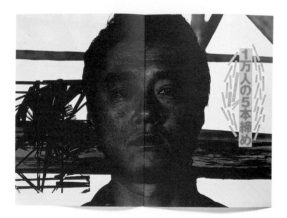

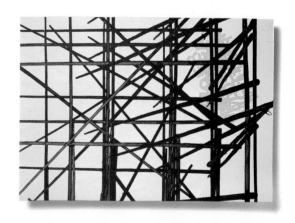

JT SUPER SOUND '89
JT スーパーサウンド '89

JAPAN 1989

Creative Director

Shigeo Goto

Art Director

Kouichi Hara

Designers

Takashi Igarashi

Eiichi Shimazaki

Photographer

Katsuo Hanzawa

Copywriter

Shigeo Goto

Design Firm

Trout

Client

Japan Tabacco

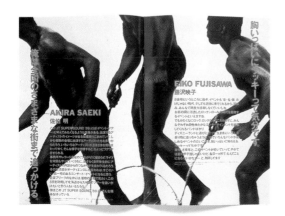

ACADEMY OF ART'S CONTEST
"CRANBROOK IN JAPAN"
美術大学の作品展
"CRANBROOK IN JAPAN"

JAPAN 1991

Art Director

Ryoji Ohashi

Designer

Ryoji Ohashi

Photographer

Takashi Yato

Design Firm

Sugarpot GR

Client

**Executive Committee of
Cranbrook in Japan**

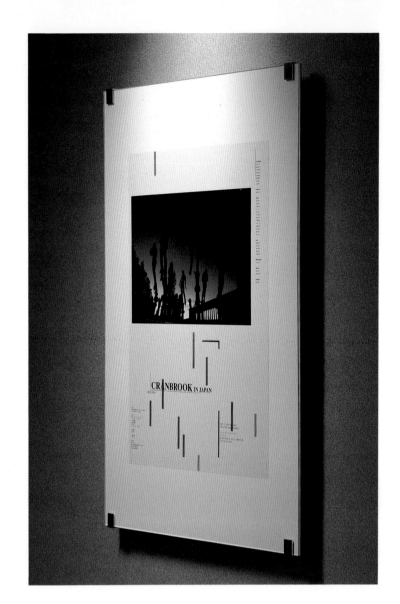

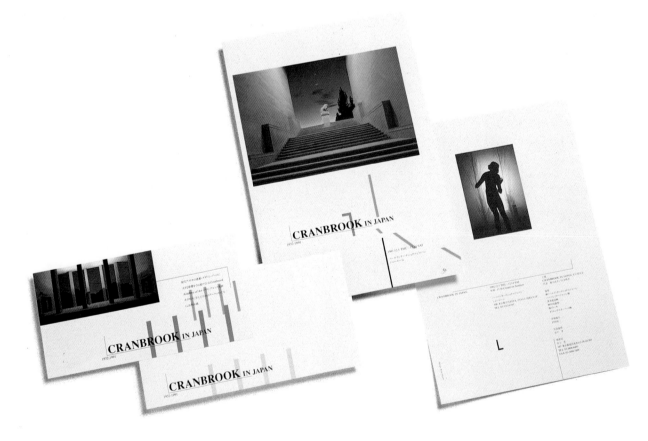

DESIGN COMPETITION
"STOP DREAMING"
デザインコンペティション
"STOP DREAMING"

USA 1985

Art Director

Jack Anderson

Designers

Jack Anderson

Rick Hess

Illustrator

Nancy Gellos

Design Firm

Hornall Anderson Design Works

Client

Seattle Design Association

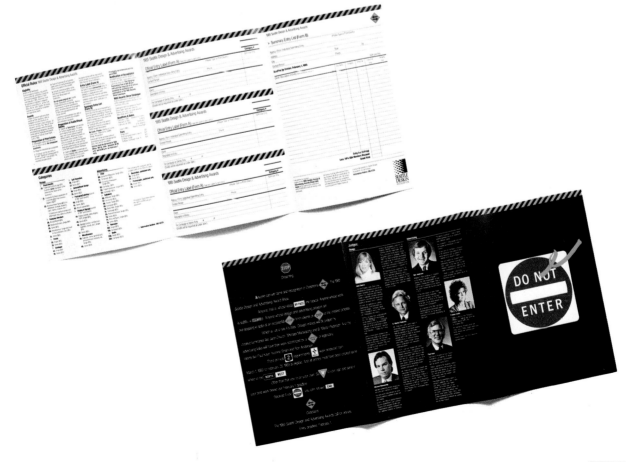

AIGA T-SHIRT CONTEST
AIGA Tシャツ コンテスト

USA 1992

Art Director

Charles S. Anderson

Designers

Charles S. Anderson

Todd Hauswirth

Daniel Olson

Illustrators

Various

Copywriters

Lisa Pemrick

Todd Hauswirth

Design Firm

Charles S. Anderson Design

Client

AIGA National New York, NY

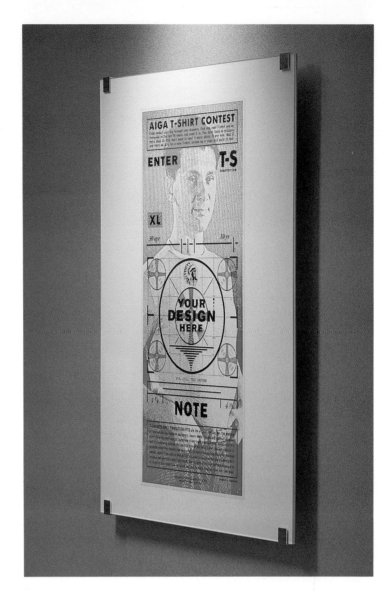

PHOTOGRAPHIC
COMPETITION AND EXHIBITION
"OTTAWA'S OTTAWA"
写真コンペティションと展示会
"OTTAWA'S OTTAWA"

CANADA 1991

Art Director
Mark Timmings

Designer
Daniel Lohnes

Photographer
Martin Lipman

Design Firm
Turquoise Design

Client
Urban Photographic Project

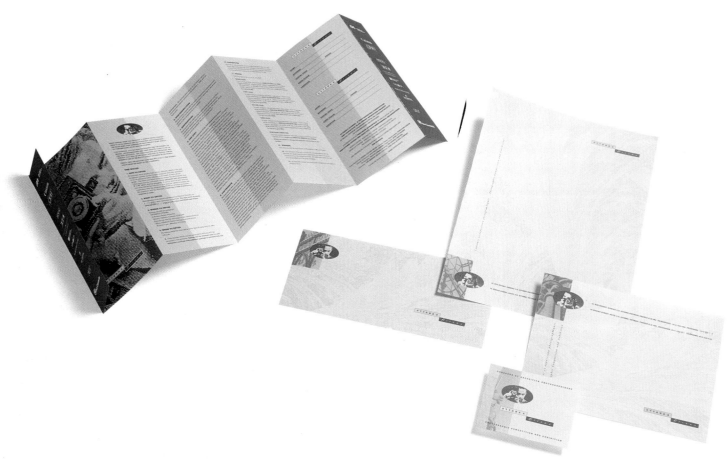

COMPETITION
"DESIGNERS SATURDAY"
コンペティション
"DESIGNERS SATURDAY"

AUSTRALIA 1992

Creative Director

Garry Emery

Art Director

Emery Vincent Associates

Designer

Emery Vincent Associates

Photographer

Emery Vincent Associates

Illustrator

Emery Vincent Associates

Copywriter

Emery Vincent Associates

Design Firm

Emery Vincent Associates

Client

Carmen Furniture (sales)

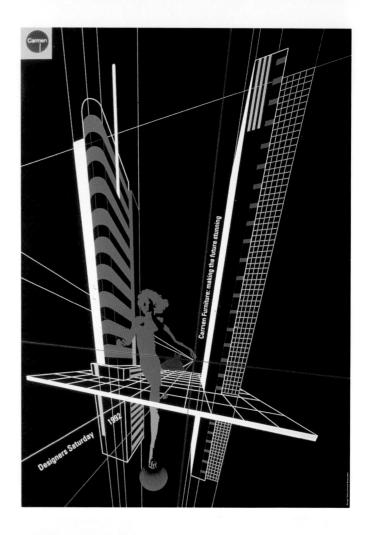

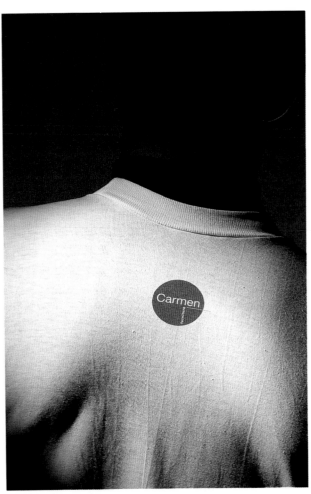

NEW-JAPAN TYPOGRAPHY
第12回石井賞
創作タイプフェイスコンテスト展

JAPAN 1992

Art Director

Katsumi Asaba

Designer

Keiko Mineishi

Photographers

Kazumi Kurigami

Toshiaki Takeuchi

Copywriter

Takako Terunuma

Mark Designer

Masamichi Suzuki

Design Firm

Asaba Design

Client

Shaken

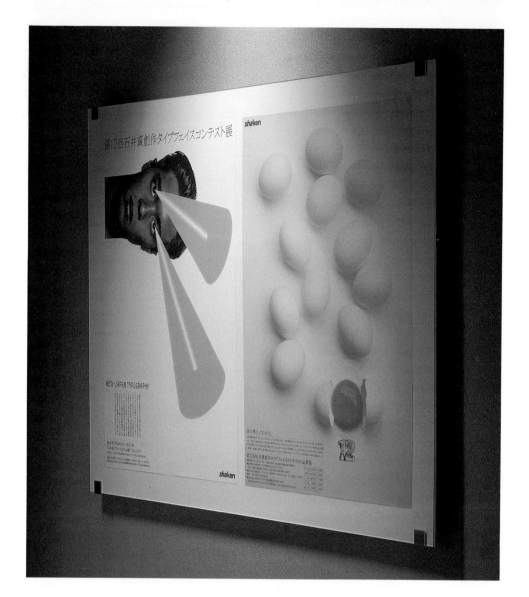

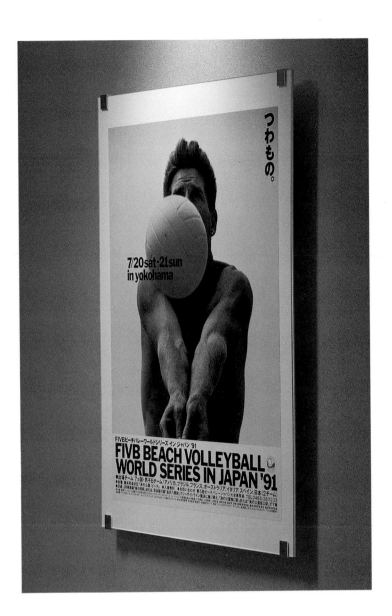

FIVB BEACH VOLLEYBALL
WORLD SERIES IN JAPAN '91
ビーチバレー ワールドシリーズ
イン ジャパン '91

JAPAN 1991

Art Director

Kiyotaka Ichikawa

Designer

Yuki Kaneda

Photographer

Masaaki Ohtake

Copywriter

Masayuki Minoda

Design Firm

Minami Aoyama Jimusho

Client

FIVB

JAPAN 1992

Creative Directors

Ichiro Kumakura

Shigeki Motoyama

Art Director

Tadanori Yokoo

Designer

Takahiro Eguchi

Illustrator

Tadanori Yokoo

Design Firms

Tadanori Yokoo Atelier

T-Break

Client

PIA

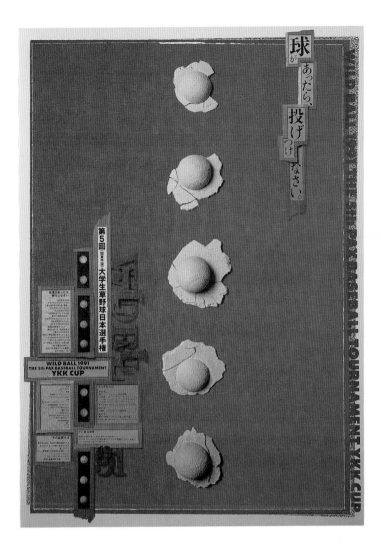

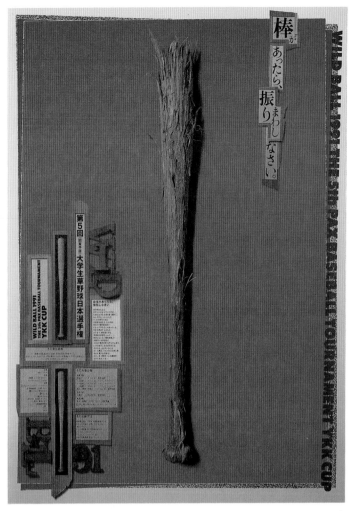

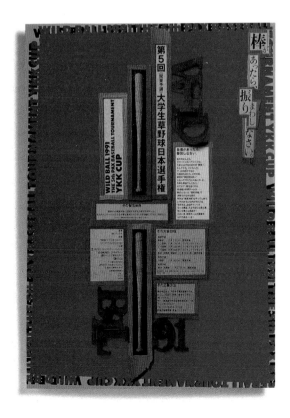

WILD BALL 1991 YKK CUP
第5回大学生草野球日本選手権

JAPAN 1991

Creative Director

Toru Takahashi

Art Director

Jun Takechi

Designer

Jun Takechi

Photographer

Masato Tokiwa

Copywriter

Manabu Goto

Object Designer

Jun Takechi

Design Firm

Verve

Clients

Pax

YKK

THE TABLE TENNIS
ザ・卓球

JAPAN 1990

Art Director

Katsumi Asaba

Designer

Teruo Kataoka

Photographer

Naruyasu Nabeshima

Copywriter

Jun Maki

Object Designer

Hiroshi Tomura

Design Firm

Asaba Design

Client

Japan Table Tennis Association

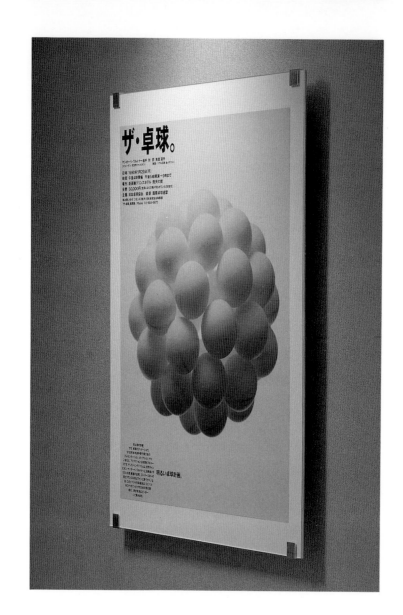

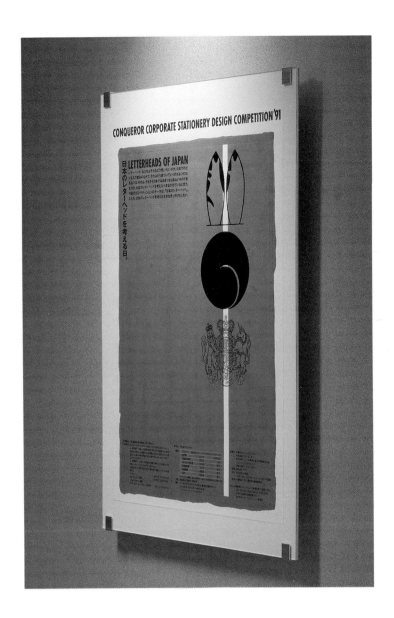

CONQUEROR CORPORATE
STATIONERY DESIGN
COMPETITION '91
コンケラー'91
日本のレターヘッドを考える日

JAPAN 1991

Art Director

Katsumi Asaba

Designer

Shirohide Azuma

Illustrator

Shinya Fukatsu

Copywriter

Haruki Nagumo

Design Firm

Asaba Design

Client

Yamato

5th KOIZUMI INTERNATIONAL LIGHTING DESIGN COMPETITION FOR STUDENTS
第5回国際学生照明デザイン
コンペティション

JAPAN 1991

Art Director

Koichi Sato

Designer

Koichi Sato

Client

Koizumi Sangyo

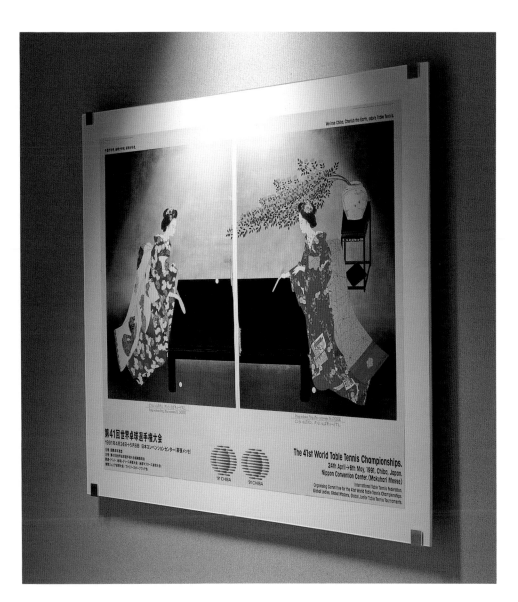

THE 41st WORLD TABLE TENNIS
CHAMPIONSHIPS
第41回世界卓球選手権大会

JAPAN 1991

Art Director

Katsumi Asaba

Designer

Teruo Kataoka

Illustrator

Tei Nakamura

Copywriter

Shigesato Itoi

Design Firm

Asaba Design

Client

**International Table Tennis
Federation**

**MARATHON
"DUKE CITY MARATHON 1992"**
マラソン
"DUKE CITY MARATHON 1992"

USA 1992

Art Director

Rick Vaughn

Designer

Rick Vaughn

Illustrator

Rick Vaughn

Design Firm

Vaughn / Wedeen Creative

Client

Duke City Marathon

PROMOTION FOR
GLOBAL SOLIDARITY FROM
THE POLISH PAVILION AT EXPO '92
"EARTH FLAG"

'92 セビリア万博の
ポーランド館における全世界の
連帯を呼びかけるプロモーション
"EARTH FLAG"

UK 1991

Art Director

Mervyn Kurlansky

Designer

Mervyn Kurlansky

Design Firm

Pentagram Design

Client

Polish Government

PROMOTION FOR
GLOBAL SOLIDARITY BY
THE POLISH GOVERMENT
"EARTH FLAG"

全世界の連帯を呼びかける
ポーランド政府による
プロモーション
"EARTH FLAG"

UK 1991

Art Director

John Mcconnell

Designer

John Mcconnell

Design Firm

Pentagram Design

Client

Polish Government

UNITED WAY
FUNDRAISING CAMPAIGN
"TOPPING THE CHARTS"
ユナイテッド・ウェイ
資金集めキャンペーン
"TOPPING THE CHARTS"

USA 1991

Art Director

Eric Rickabaugh

Designer

Eric Rickabaugh

Illustrator

Mike Linley

Design Firm

Rickabaugh Graphics

Client

Huntington Banks

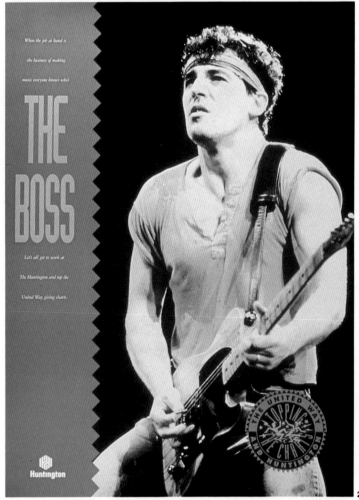

Item
1. Poster
2. Poster
3. Gift box contents
4. T-shirt
5. Letterhead
6. Invitation card
7. Gift box card

3

4

5

6

7

**FUNDRAISING CAMPAIGN OF
ARCHITECTURE DESIGN OFFICE
"NBBJ-1991 UNITED WAY
FUNDRAISING CAMPAIGN"**
建築デザイン事務所の
資金集めキャンペーン
"NBBJ-1991 UNITED WAY
FUNDRAISING CAMPAIGN"

USA 1991

Creative Director

Kerry Burg

Art Director

Designer

Klindt Parker

Photographers

Various

Illustrator

Klindt Parker

Copywriters

Klindt Parker

Susan Dewey

Design Firm

NBBJ-Graphic Design

Client

NBBJ-Seattle

FUNDRAISER FOR
THE ALZHEIMER ASSOCIATION
"COMEBACK"
アルツハイマー病協会の
資金集め活動
"COMEBACK"

USA 1991

Art Directors

Mark Krumel

Designers

Mark Krumel

Mike Smith

Eric Rickabaugh

Photographer

Larry Hamill

Illustrator

Tony Meuser

Copywriter

Steve Shivinsky

Design Firm

Rickabaugh Graphics

Client

The Alzheimer's Association

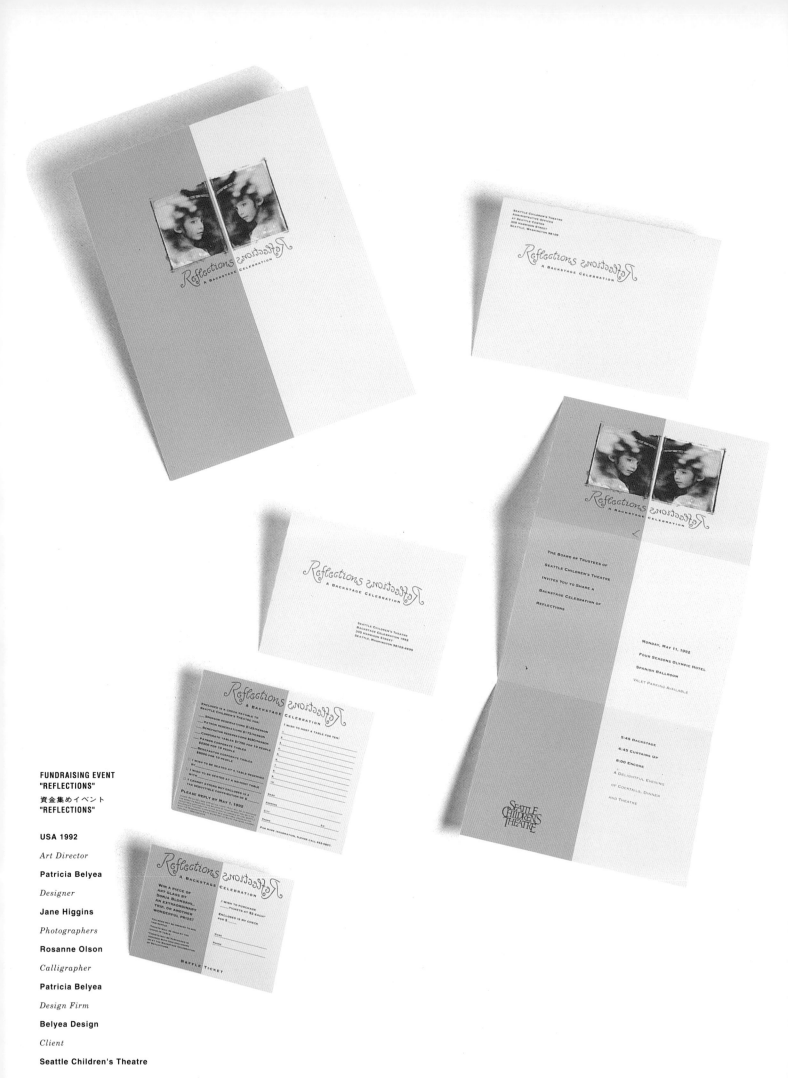

FUNDRAISING EVENT
"REFLECTIONS"
資金集めイベント
"REFLECTIONS"

USA 1992

Art Director

Patricia Belyea

Designer

Jane Higgins

Photographers

Rosanne Olson

Calligrapher

Patricia Belyea

Design Firm

Belyea Design

Client

Seattle Children's Theatre

NON-PROFIT EVENT
"DANCES FOR 30TH STREET"
ノン・プロフィット イベント
"DANCES FOR 30TH STREET"

USA 1991

Creative Director

Gail Rigelhaupt

Designer

Gail Rigelhaupt

Photographers

Robert D. Golding

Beatrr Schiller

Copywriter

Elise Bernhardt

Design Firm

Rigelhaupt Design

Client

Dancing In The Streets

ALZHEIMER'S CHARITY GOLF 1990

1990 アルツハイマー病協会の
チャリティ・ゴルフ

USA 1990

Creative Directors

Ron Sullivan

Mark Perkins

Art Director

Jon Flaming

Designer

Jon Flaming

Illustrator

Jon Flaming

Copywriter

Janiece Upshaw

Design Firm

Sullivan Perkins

Client

The Alzheimer's Association

ALZHEIMER'S CHARITY GOLF 1991

1991 アルツハイマー病協会の
チャリティ・ゴルフ

USA 1991

Creative Directors

Ron Sullivan

Mark Perkins

Art Director

Jon Flaming

Designer

Jon Flaming

Illustrator

Jon Flaming

Copywriter

Janiece Upshaw

Design Firm

Sullivan Perkins

Client

The Alzheimer's Association

精神医療協会の子供達のための
チャリティテニス
"SHOOT OUT 1990"

USA 1990

Creative Directors

Ron Sullivan

Mark Perkins

Art Director

Art Garcia

Designer

Art Garcia

Illustrator

Art Garcia

Copywriters

Mark Perkins

Sherry Landa

Design Firm

Sullivan Perkins

Client

**Mental Health Association of
Dallas County**

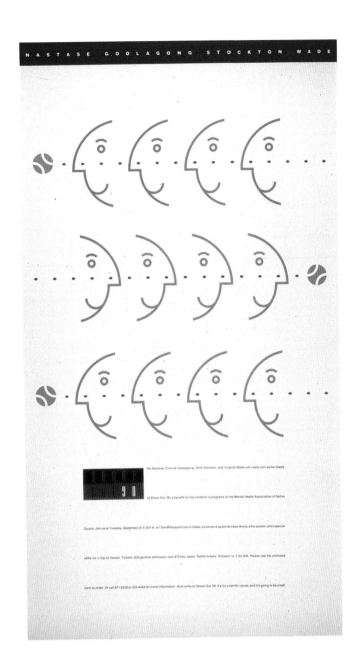

精神医療協会の子供達のための
チャリティテニス
"SHOOT OUT 1991"

USA 1991

Creative Directors

Ron Sullivan

Mark Perkins

Art Director

Art Garcia

Designer

Art Garcia

Photographer

Jeff Covington

Copywriters

Mark Perkins

Hilary Proctor

Design Firm

Sullivan Perkins

Client

**Mental Health Association of
Dallas County**

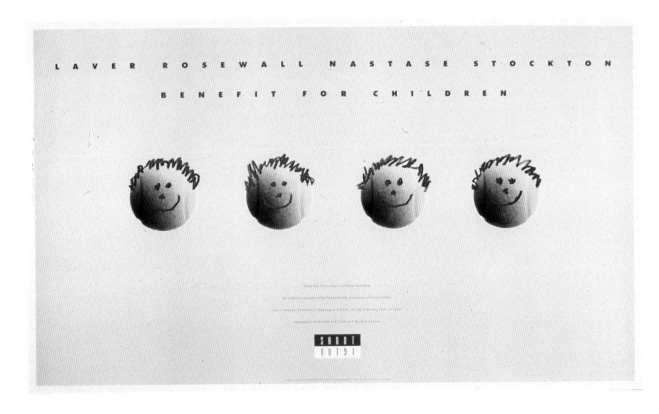

NATIONAL CONDOM WEEK
全国コンドーム週間

USA 1992

Creative Director

Tommer Peterson

Art Director

James Forkner

Designers

James Forkner

Dan Baker

Illustrator

James Forkner

Copywriters

Tommer Peterson

Rich Lindsay

Design Firm

Wilkins & Peterson

Client

Northwest AIDS Foundation

NATIONAL CONDOM WEEK
"KEEP IT UP SEATTLE"
全国コンドーム週間
"KEEP IT UP SEATTLE"

USA 1990

Art Directors

Tommer Peterson

Warren Wilkins

Designer

Craig Kelley

Illustrator

Craig Kelley

Design Firm

Wilkins & Peterson

Client

Northwest AIDS Foundation

NON-PROFIT DINNER
ノン・プロフィットディナー

USA 1992

Art Director

Carlos Segura

Designer

Carlos Segura

Illustrator

Mary Flock Lempa

Copywriter

Alan Gandelman

Design Firm

Segura

Client

The Menomonee Club

**FUNDRAISING FESTIVAL
"A VERY SPECIAL
RASPBERRY SUNDAY"**
資金集めのフェスティバル
**"A VERY SPECIAL
RASPBERRY SUNDAY"**

USA 1991

Art Director

Eric Rickabaugh

Designer

Tina Zientarski

Illustrator

Evangelia Philippidis

Design Firm

Rickabaugh Graphics

Client

Very Special Arts Ohio

EVENT OF NON-PROFIT
FUNDRAISING ORGANIZATION
"ORCHID LIGHTS"
募金団体の資金集めイベント
"ORCHID LIGHTS"

USA 1992

Art Director

Haley Johnson

Designer

Haley Johnson

Illustrator

Haley Johnson

Copywriter

Jan Goldsmith

Design Firm

Charles S. Anderson Design

Client

**Minnesota Landscape
Arboretum**

CHARITY BENEFIT OF
A FOOD MARKET
"GRAND GOURMET GALA"
食品マーケットのチャリティ事業
"GRAND GOURMET GALA"

USA 1991

Creative Director

Linda Natal

Designer

Tracy Sabin

Illustrator

Tracy Sabin

Design Firm

Sabin Design

Client

Horton Plaza Farmer's Market

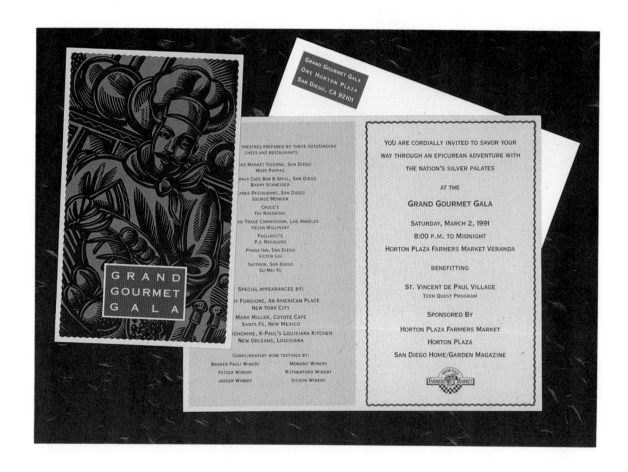

Submitors' Index

EDITORIAL CREDITS

Art Director

Kazuo Abe　阿部かずお

Designers

Sinji Ikenoue　池之上信二

Kimiko Ishiwatari　石渡君子

Yutaka Ichimura　市村　裕

Editors

Kaori Shibata　柴田かおり

Kazuhisa Yoshihara　吉原和久

Photographer

Fujimoto Kuniharu　藤本邦治

English Translator & Adviser

Write Away Co., Ltd.　ライトアウエイ

Publisher

Shingo Miyoshi　三芳伸吾**

Special Event Graphics

1992年12月12日初版第1版発行

発行所　ピエ・ブックス

〒170 東京都豊島区駒込4-14-6-407

TEL: 03-3949-5010

FAX: 03-3949-5650

製版・印刷・製本　弘陽印刷

〒116 東京都荒川区東日暮里4－8－12

TEL: 03-3802-1221 FAX: 03-3801-9388

ISBN 4-938586-35-5　C3070 P16000E

P·I·E Books, as always, has several new and ambitious graphic book projects in the works which will introduce a variety of superior designs from Japan and abroad. Currently we are planning the collection series detailed below. If you have any graphics which you consider worthy for submission to these publications, please fill in the necessary information on the inserted questionnaire postcard and forward it to us. You will receive a notice when the relevant project goes into production.

ピエ・ブックスでは、今後も新しいタイプの
グラフィック書籍の出版を目指すとともに、
国内外の優れたデザインを幅広く
紹介していきたいと考えております。
今後の刊行予定として下記のコレクション・シリーズを
企画しておりますので、
作品提供していただける企画がございましたら、
挟み込みのアンケートハガキに必要事項を記入の上
お送り下さい。企画が近づきましたら
そのつど案内書をお送りいたします。

A. POSTCARD GRAPHICS

A collection of various types of postcards including product advertising, direct mailers, invitations to events such as parties and fashion shows as well as birthday cards and seasonal greetings. In short all sorts of cards except the letter type which are mailed in envelopes.

A. ポストカード・グラフィックス

各シーズンのグリーティングカードをはじめとして、商品広告DM、パーティーやコレクション等のイベントのお知らせ、バースデイカードなど封書タイプを除く様々なポストカードをコレクションします。

B. ADVERTISING GREETING CARDS

A collection of letter-style direct mailers including sales promotional sheets, invitations to events such as exhibitions, parties and weddings. Some of these are quite simple, some have unusual shapes or dimensions (limited to cards inserted in envelopes).

B. アドバタイジング・グリーティングカード

販促用のDM、展示会・イベントの案内状やパーティや結婚式などの招待状など、プレーンなものから形状の変わったもの・立体になったものまで封書タイプのDMをコレクションします。（封書タイプのものに限ります）

C. BROCHURE & PAMPHLET COLLECTION

A collection of brochures and pamphlets categorized according to the business of the client company. Includes sales promotional pamphlets, product catalogues, corporate image brochures gallery exhibitions, special events, annual reports and company profiles from all sorts of businesses.

C. ブローシュア & パンフレット・コレクション

販促用パンフレット、商品カタログ、イメージ・カタログ、ギャラリーや展示会・イベントのパンフレット、アニュアル・リポート、会社案内など様々な業種のブローシュアやパンフレットを業種別にコレクションします。

D. POSTER GRAPHICS

A collection of posters, classified according to the business of the client. Fashion, department stores, automotive, food, home appliances and almost any sort of poster you might see on streets. Invitational posters for art exhibitions, concerts and plays as well as regional posters which will be seen for the first time outside of the local area where they were published.

D. ポスター・グラフィックス

ファッション、デパート、車、食品、家電など街角を飾る広告ポスター、美術展、コンサート、演劇などのイベント案内ポスター、見る機会の少ない地方のポスターなどを業種別にコレクションします。

E. BOOK COVER AND EDITORIAL DESIGNS

Editorial and cover designs for various types of books and magazines. Includes all sorts of magazines, books, comics and other visual publications.

E. ブックカバー & エディトリアル・デザイン

雑誌、単行本、ヴィジュアル書、コミックなど様々なタイプの書籍・雑誌のエディトリアル・デザイン、カバー・デザインを紹介します。

F. CORPORATE IMAGE LOGO DESIGNS

A collection of C.I. materials mainly symbols and logos for corporations of all sorts, classified according to the type of business. In some cases, development samples and trial comps as well as the final designs are included. Includes logos for magazines and various products.

F. コーポレイト・イメージ・ロゴマーク・デザイン

企業やショップのシンボルマーク・ロゴマークを中心に幅広い業種にわたり分類しコレクションします。マークのみではなく展開例としてのアプリケーションも数多く紹介し、その他、雑誌や商品などの様々なロゴマークもコレクションします。

G. BUSINESS CARD AND LETTERHEAD GRAPHICS

A collection of cards such as the business cards of corporations and individuals as well as shopping cards for restaurants and boutiques, membership cards and various prepaid cards. This collection centers on business cards, letterheads and shopping cards of superior design.

G. ビジネスカード & レターヘッド・グラフィックス

様々な企業や個人の名刺、レストランやブティックのショップカード、会員カード、プリペイドカードなど、デザイン的に優れたカードを名刺・ショップカードを中心にコレクション。またカードのみでなくレターヘッドも紹介します。

H. CALENDAR GRAPHICS

A collection of visually interesting calendars. We do not take into account the form of the calendar, i.e. wall hanging-type or note-type or desktop-type etc. So that the calendars represent the widest range of possibilities.

H. カレンダー・グラフィックス

ヴィジュアル的に優れたカレンダーをコレクションします。壁掛けタイプ、ノートタイプ、ダイアリー、日めくりタイプ、卓上タイプなど形状にはこだわらず幅広い分野の様々なタイプのカレンダーを紹介します。

I. PACKAGE AND WRAPPING GRAPHICS

A collection of packaging and wrapping materials of superior design from Japan and abroad. Includes related accessories such as labels and ribbons and almost anything else that comes under the heading of containing, protecting and decorating things.

I. パッケージ & ラッピング・グラフィックス

商品そのもののパッケージデザインはもちろん、いろいろな物を包む、保護する、飾るというコンセプトで国内外の優れたパッケージ、ケース、ラッピング・デザイン及びラベル、リボンなどの付属アクセサリー類を幅広く紹介します。

Comme toujours, P·I·E Books a dans ses ateliers plusieurs projets de livres graphiques neufs et ambitieux qui introduiront une gamme de modèles supérieurs en provenance du Japon et de l'étranger. Nous prévoyons en ce moment la série de collections détaillée cidessous. Si vous êtes en possession d'un graphique que vous jugez digne de soumettre à ces publications, nous vous prions de remplir les informations nécessaires sur l'étiquette à renvoyer située à la carte postale questionnaire insérée et de nous la faire parvenir. Vous recevrez un avis lorsque le projet correspondant passera à la production.

Wie immer hat P·I·E Books einige neue anspruchsvolle Grafikbücher in Arbeit, die eine Vielzahl von hervorragenden Designs aus Japan und anderen Ländern vorstellen werden. Momentan planen wir eine Serie mit den nachfolgend aufgeführten Themen.
Wenn Sie grafische Darstellungen besitzen, von denen Sie meinen, daß sie in diese Veröffentlichung aufgenommen werden könnten, geben Sie uns bitte die nötigen Informationen auf der entsprechenden Antwortseite am füllen Sie die beigelegte Antwortkarte aus und schicken Sie sie an uns. Wir werden Sie benachrichtigen, wenn das entsprechende Projekt in Arbeit geht.

A. Graphiques pour cartes postales
Une collection de divers types de cartes postales, y compris la publicité de produits, l'adressage direct, des invitations à des événements tels que soirées et défilés de mode, ainsi que des cartes d'anniversaire et des voeux de saison. En bref, toutes sortes de cartes, à part le type lettre qui sera envoyé dans des enveloppes.

A. Postkarten-Grafik
Zusammenstellung verschiedener Postkartenarten, und zwar für Produktwerbung, Direct Mailing, Einladungen zu Parties und Modenschauen sowie Geburtstagskarten und Karten zu verschiedenen Jahreszeiten. Also alle Arten von Karten, ausgenommen Briefkarten.

B. Cartes de voeux publicitaires
Une collection d'adressages directs style lettre y compris des feuilles de promotion de ventes, des invitations à des événements tels qu'expositions, soirées et mariages. Certaines d'entre elles sont très simples, d'autres ont des formes ou dimensions inhabituelles (limitées aux cartes insérées dans des enveloppes).

B. Werbe-Grußkarten
Zusammenstellung briefähnlicher Direct-Mailings, wie z.B. verkaufsfördernde Texte, Einladungen zu Anlässen wie Ausstellungen, Parties oder Hochzeiten. Einige von ihnen sind recht einfach gemacht, andere fallen durch ungewöhnliches Aussehen oder Größe auf (Karten dürfen Umschlaggröße nicht überschreiten).

C. Collection de brochures et de pamphlets
Une collection de brochures et de pamphlets triées en fonction des affaires de la société client. Comprend des pamphlets de promotion des ventes, des catalogues de produits, des brochures sur l'image de la société, des expositions de galerie, des événements spéciaux, des compte-rendus annuels et des profils de sociétés de toutes sortes d'affaires.

C. Zusammenstellung von Broschüren und Druckschriften
Diese Zusammenstellung von Broschüren und Druckschriften ist nach den Tätigkeiten der Kundenfirmen geordnet. Sie beinhaltet verkaufsfördernde Broschüren, Produktkataloge, Corporate-Image-Broschüren, Galerieausstellungen, besondere Veranstaltungen und Firmenprofile für alle Arten von Unternehmen.

D. Graphiques sur affiche
Une collection d'affiches, classées en fonction du secteur d'affaires du client. La mode, les grands magasins, l'automobile, l'alimentation, les appareils électro-ménagers et presque tous les types d'affiche que vous pouvez voir dans les rues. Des affiches invitant à des expositions d'art, des concerts et des pièces ainsi que des affiches régionales qui seront vues pour la première fois en dehors de la région où elles ont été éditées.

D. Postergrafik
Eine Zusammenstellung von Postern, die nach dem Geschäftsgebiet des Kunden geordnet sind. Mode Kaufhäuser, Kraftfahrzeuge, Nahrungsmittel, Haushaltsgeräte und fast jede Art von Postern, die auf der Straße zu sehen sind. Einladungsposter für Kunstausstellungen, Konzerte und Theaterstücke ebenso wie Poster mit regionalen Themen, die zum ersten Mal außerhalb des Gebietes, in dem sie aufgehängt wurden, zu sehen sein werden.

E. Designs de couverture de livre et d'éditorial
Des designs de livre et d'éditorial de divers types de livres et magazines. Comprend toutes sortes de magazines, livres, bandes dessinées et autres publications visuelles.

E. Bucheinbände und redaktionelles Design
Bucheinbände und redaktionelles Design für verschiedenste Buch- und Zeitschriftentypen. Dies schließt alle Arten von Zeitschriften, Büchern, Comics und anderen visuellen Publikationen ein.

F. Designs de logo d'image de société
Une collection de matériaux d'image de société, principalement des symboles et des logos pour sociétés de toutes sortes ; classés en fonction du type d'affaires. Dans certains cas, sont inclus des échantillons de développement et également des compositions d'essai ainsi que les designs finaux. Comprend des logos pour magazines et divers produits.

F. Corporate-Image-Logo-Design
Dies ist eine Zusammenstellung von C.I.-Material, und zwar hauptsächlich von Symbolen und Logos für Firmen aller Art, nach Geschäftsgebieten geordnet. In manchen Fällen sind die Arbeiten der Entwicklungsphase und Probeexemplare ebenso miteinbezogen wie das endgültige Design. Logos für Zeitschriften und andere Produkte sind miteingeschlossen.

G. Graphiques pour en-têtes et cartes de visite
Une collection de cartes telles que les cartes de visite de sociétés et d'individus ainsi que les cartes de fidélité de restaurants et de boutiques, les cartes de membre et diverses cartes payées à l'avance. Cette collection se concentre sur les cartes de visite, les en-têtes et les cartes de fidélité d'une qualité supérieure.

G. Visitenkarten und Briefkopf-Grafik
Dies ist eine Zusammenstellung verschiedener Visitenkarten, z.B. für Firmen und Einzelpersonen, Kreditkarten für Restaurants und Boutiquen, Mitgliedskarten und Vorverkaufskarten. Diese Sammlung konzentriert sich vor allem auf geschäftliche Karten, Briefköpfe und Geschäftseigene Kreditkarten mit herausragendem Design.

H. Graphiques pour calendrier
Une collection de calendriers visuellement intéressants. Nous ne tenons pas compte de la forme du calendrier, c.-à-d., type à accrocher au mur, type carnet ou type bureau, etc. de telle sorte que les calendriers représentent la gamme de possibilités la plus large.

H. Kalendergrafik
Eine Zusammenstellung von optisch interessanten Kalendern. Es ist für uns dabei unwichtig, ob es sich um die Form des Wandkalenders, Tischkalenders oder Notizbuchkalenders handelt, sodaß die größtmögliche Vielfalt an Kalendern gezeigt werden kann.

I. Graphiques pour emballage et paquetage
Une collection de matériaux d'emballage et de paquetage de qualité supérieure en provenance du Japon et de l'étranger. Comprend des accessoires en relation tels qu'étiquettes et rubans, et presque tout ce qui est destiné à contenir, protéger et décorer des choses.

I. Grafik auf Verpackungen und Verpackungsmaterial
Eine Zusammenstellung von Grafik auf Verpackungen und Verpackungsmaterial mit herausragendem Design aus Japan und anderen Ländern. Dazugehörige Accessoires wie Etiketten und Bänder sind eingeschlossen, ebenso wie fast alles, was als Behälter für Produkte dienen kann, sie ziert oder schützt.

P·I·E BOOKS

NEW TITLES

GRAPHIC BEAT / LONDON-TOKYO Vol: 1 & 2

Pages: 224 (208 in color) Format: 225mm x 300mm

Binding: Hardbound with jacket Pub.date: Vol: 1 & 2: Available now

"The GRAPHIC BEAT" presents a compilation of graphic art created by 17 London and 12 Tokyo graphic designers who are continually breaking new ground, doing much to influence internationally the graphic trends of the past few years. Each designer has contibuted work not just in music but in all areas of design; posters, logotypes, catalogues, magazines and perhaps most importantly their personal expressions of art; Graphic or not. Features Malcolm Garrett, Russell Mills, Tadanori Yokoo, Peter Saville, Hajime Tachibana, Terry Jones, Neville Brody, Mic*Itaya, Garry Mouat, Yukimasa Okumura, Jamie Reid, Vaughan Oliver and many more.

CALENDAR GRAPHICS

Pages: 224 (192 in color) Format: 225mm x 300mm Binding: Hardbound with jacket Pub. date: Available now

Featuring approximately 250 calendars carefully selected from 500 entries produced in Japan and 20 other countries.

This book presents various types of calendars collected both from Japan and overseas. The formats include poster-type, book-type, daily and monthly tear-off types and even various 3-dimensional specialty calendars. Also featured are original collections from art museums which have not previously been shown widely, and calendars which can only be considered objets d'art. There are "POP" calendars, produced as music promotion graphics and commercially available calendars which are sold everywhere. In short, an unlimited variety. This book will afford you the boundless pleasure of leafing through some of the finest, most original calendar art ever created.

The Creative Index ARTIFILE Vol. 1

Pages: 224 (192 in color) Format: 225mm x 300mm Binding: Hardbound with jacket Pub. date: Available now

This first edition of ARTIFILE showcases the best works from 104 top graphic design studios from Japan and abroad. A variety of fields have been included such as advertising design, corporate identity, photography and illustration. All works are presented in striking full-color and include comments from the designers themselves. This annual publication is the perfect visual resource for all graphic designers looking for new perspectives.

BUSINESS CARD GRAPHICS 2

Pages: 224 (192 in color) Format: 225mm x 300mm Binding: Hardbound with jacket Pub. date: Available now

As an encore to the original BUSINESS CARD GRAPHICS, this new international collection presents 1,000 business cards selected on the basis of excellence in design. Emphasis has been given to cards used in creative fields such as graphic design and architecture. These exciting, trend-setting works are sure to be a source of inspiration for graphic designers and art directors.

T-Shirt GRAPHICS

Pages: 224 (192 in color) Format: 225mm x 300mm Binding: Hardbound with jacket Pub. date: Available now

Cool and casual, artistic and expressive, commercial & promotional...T-shirts, the garment of choice for millions, are all of these and more. Emblazoned with more than just a catch phrase or trendy design, T-shirts are an important promotional item bearing logos and brand names of corporations large and small.

The editors at P.I.E BOOKS showcase the entire spectrum of T-shirt graphics with this delightful collection of shirts gatherd from top designers worldwide. Categories include casual and designer T-shirts, shirts promoting exhibitions, concerts and events, shirts bearing logos, trademarks and brand names, self-promotional shirts from design agencies and others from schools, museums and organizations. Some 700 glorious designs in all, most in full-color.

T-SHIRT GRAPHICS is a valuable and inspirational visual sourcebook for all graphic and textile designers and also for corporate communications and C.I. specialist.